Richard Maurice Bucke

Man's Moral Nature

Richard Maurice Bucke
Man's Moral Nature
ISBN/EAN: 9783337022846
Printed in Europe, USA, Canada, Australia, Japan
Cover: Foto ©Suzi / pixelio.de

More available books at **www.hansebooks.com**

MAN'S

MORAL NATURE

AN ESSAY

BY
RICHARD MAURICE BUCKE, M.D.

MEDICAL SUPERINTENDENT OF THE ASYLUM FOR
THE INSANE, LONDON, ONTARIO

"*I am a man who is preoccupied of his own soul.*"

NEW YORK
G. P. PUTNAM'S SONS
TORONTO, ONT.: WILLING & WILLIAMSON
1879

[*All Rights Reserved*]

I DEDICATE THIS BOOK TO THE MAN WHO INSPIRED IT—TO THE MAN WHO OF ALL MEN PAST AND PRESENT THAT I HAVE KNOWN HAS THE MOST EXALTED MORAL NATURE—

TO

WALT WHITMAN.

SOCRATES: "But the difficulty begins as soon as we raise the question whether these principles are three or one; whether, that is to say, we learn with one part of our nature, are angry with another, and with a third part desire the satisfaction of our natural appetites; or whether the whole soul comes into play in each sort of action:—to determine that is the difficulty."

GLAUCON: "Yes, there lies the difficulty."

SOCRATES: "Then let us now try and determine whether they are the same or different."

JOWETT'S PLATO, REP.

ADVERTISEMENT.

No conclusion in this book is considered by its Author as absolute or even certain; the book is simply a record of the way things look to him. The series of thoughts which gave rise to it was involuntary and irrepressible. To write these down and formulate them was not a choice but a necessity. The Author cannot therefore claim that he writes the book to make the world wiser. He certainly does not write it for money or fame, neither does he look for either as his reward—in fact he is far from being certain that he deserves any reward; but if he succeeds in relieving his own mind of some of the problems which have weighed upon it for more than twenty years, he will consider himself well paid; and should he also succeed in transplanting some of these problems into other and better minds, where they may reach a higher development and receive a truer, a more perfect solution, this would be a compensation indeed—not for writing the book, which was not a labor and needed no compensation, but for the years of mental travail that these problems have imposed upon him.

TO THE READER.

THIS book has been not so much written as it has grown. "Backward I see in my own days where I sweated through fog with linguists and contenders;" but that was before this book began; at present, "I have no mockings and arguments—I witness and wait." The thought grew and its shadow fell on the paper, *voilà tout*. As long ago as I can recollect, the questions discussed in this essay—the nature of good and evil—the causes and proportions of happiness and unhappiness — whether mankind was getting better or worse—what is the meaning of vice and virtue—and whether there were such things in nature as rewards and punishments—and if so what these meant—these questions and others allied to them continually seemed to demand some answer. They received many answers which were in turn accepted and discarded. But the soil was being prepared by this constant growth and decomposition of ideas, just as is the material soil by the constant growth and disintegration of vegetable forms for the growth of higher species. At last—years ago now—a THOUGHT pushed upward through this soil thus prepared. I knew at once that this thought contained what I had so long looked for—it contained it as the acorn contains the oak. The acorn contains the oak, but the oak is not in the acorn—so the thought contained the solution, but the solution was not in the thought. The thought grew—it put out leaves and branches. It grew in me, but I had nothing to do with it—I had absolutely no control over it. It has grown into this book as independently of my volition as the oak is independent of the will of the soil. The chapters of the book are its branches, and the words are its leaves. It seemed to me from the first, as it seems to me now, that this thought has some novelty, truth, and importance. But perhaps I am quite mistaken. I merely offer my opinion—I take no responsibility in the matter. The thought is no more mine than it is yours if you read the book and understand it. I no more made the thought than I made myself—it grew of its own accord, and now it can take care of itself; or if it cannot do that, it can do as plenty of other thoughts have done—it can die.

INTRODUCTION.

THE object of this essay is to discuss the moral nature—to point out, in the first place, its general relation to the other groups of functions belonging to, or rather making up, the individual man, and also its relations to man's environment. Secondly, to show its radical separation from these other groups of functions; then to attempt to decide of what organ it is a function—to consider whether it is a fixed quantity, or whether, like the active nature and the intellectual nature, it is in course of development. And if the moral nature is progressive, to try to find out what the essential nature of this progress is—upon what basis the progress itself rests—the direction of the progress in the past and in the future—its causes—its history—and the law of it—and to point out the conclusions which can be drawn from this progress as to the character of the universe in which we live.

CONTENTS.

CHAPTER I.
LINES OF CLEAVAGE.................................. 1

CHAPTER II.
THE MORAL NATURE AND ITS LIMITS................ 11

CHAPTER III.
THE PHYSICAL BASIS OF THE MORAL NATURE......... 45

CHAPTER IV.
IS THE MORAL NATURE A FIXED QUANTITY?......... 123

CHAPTER V.
THE HISTORY OF THE DEVELOPMENT OF THE MORAL NATURE... 157

CHAPTER VI.
THE INFERENCE TO BE DRAWN FROM THE DEVELOPMENT OF THE MORAL NATURE AS TO THE ESSENTIAL FACT OF THE UNIVERSE................................... 189

CHAPTER I.

LINES OF CLEAVAGE.

"Les régions spéculative et active du cerveau n'ont de communications nerveuses qu'avec les sens et les muscles pour apercevoir et modifier le monde exterieur. Au contraire, la region affective, qui constitue sa principale masse, n'a point de liens directs avec le dehors, auquel la rattachent indirectment ses relations propres avec l'intelligence et l'activité. Mais, outre ses liaisons cérébrales, des nerfs spéciaux la lient profondément aux principaux organes de la vie nutrition, d'après la subordination nécessaire de l'ensemble des instincts personnels à l'existence végétative."
—Auguste Comte.

ALL things, man included, are parts of one great whole. The object of this chapter is to point out the most obvious and most natural divisions of this whole, which we call the universe. These divisions can never be absolute; the whole is too truly one whole for that, but they are sufficiently real for our present purpose. The first plane of separation is between man and that which is outside man. Now, it is obvious that the external universe acts on man, and that man reacts upon and toward the external universe. The external universe acts on man through his senses; it acts on man in other ways than through his senses, but these need not be considered here. Man reacts upon and toward the external universe in three ways, namely, by his active nature; by his intellectual nature; by his moral nature— that is, he acts upon it, thinks about it, and feels toward it.

It is alone that part of the external universe which we call material which acts on man through his senses—that part of which we ordinarily feel our knowledge to be the surest; but in reality, strangely enough, as will soon appear, this is one of the aspects of the external world, of which we can know nothing. Man's receptive faculties then, his senses, correspond to only a small part of the external universe—but man's reactive faculties tally with all the external universe which is anything at all to us in our present state of existence. These considerations apply only to the dynamic or spiritual part of man, not to the static or material part. Man himself, then, pursuing the analysis we have begun, is divided, first, into structure and function—in other words, he is a static being and a dynamic being. Of this static being, however, we really have no knowledge, and its existence is open to the gravest doubt—here I shall not consider it. Did it exist it would correspond with what is called matter in the external world, but this shares the discredit of the material part of man, and will be equally unconsidered here. The first line of cleavage, then, in man, is that which may be drawn between his receptive and his reactive functions. In the external world, certain forces, such as motion, heat, and light, are correlative with man's receptive faculties, but these receptive faculties are by no means broad enough to tally with even a large part of these forces, and it is beyond a doubt that only a small part of these forces which exist immediately about us are known to us directly or indirectly. Though man's reactive functions tally far more completely with the external world than do his receptive functions, yet we shall see reason to believe, as we proceed, that these also signally fail to cover the field that is opposed to them. So far as we see at present, then, the lines of cleavage are: 1. Between man, and all that is outside man, including his fellow men. 2. Between the statical and dynamical part of man, and between the statical and dynamical aspect of the world. This is probably a false line. 3. The first line of cleavage in man himself is between his receptive and reactive functions. 4. Then the reactive functions are themselves split into three parts by the lines between the active nature and the intellectual nature, and between the intellectual nature and the moral nature. In the external world there are, as we shall see, lines of cleavage corresponding to these two last.

Man's active nature, or that part of him with which he performs all acts of which he is capable—which is represented statically by the muscles and the motor tract of the brain and cord—this part of man's nature corresponds with force in the external world. This section of the reactive functions lies on one side of the intellectual nature, as the moral nature will be seen to lie upon the other.

The intellectual nature—that part of us by which we know—which has its statical representative in the cerebrum and higher centres of the cerebro-spinal nervous system — tallies, we all know how imperfectly, with phenomena and relations of coexistence and sequence in the world which lies without us. Its principal division is into the external or receptive and registering functions of the intellect, such as perception and memory, and the internal or reflective functions, such as ratiocination and comparison. To the former correspond, in the outer world, the so-called concrete sciences, such as zoölogy, botany, geology and mineralogy. To the latter correspond the so-called abstract sciences, such as mathematics, astronomy, physics, chemistry, biology, and sociology; the relations of these to one another make up, speaking generally, what is called philosophy.

The moral nature, statically represented, as will be shown farther on, by the great sympathetic, is in relation in the outer world, not with forces nor with relations, but with qualities, and as it is certain that the active nature of man does not enter into relation with all forces, nor his intellectual nature with all relations, so it is equally certain that man's moral nature falls infinitely short of entering into relation with all qualities.

Now, to realize this division of man's reactive

functions, it must be clearly seen that, as his intellectual nature only confronts phenomena and relations, it does not confront those parts of the universe which are confronted by the active and moral natures, which is simply saying, in other language, that we know and can know nothing about force and nothing about qualities; this may seem paradoxical, but it is true. We naturally think we know something about force because we are familiar with many phenomena which we attribute to it, but a moderate amount of reflection will satisfy any candid mind that we know nothing of force itself. So with qualities. We seem to know a great deal about them, while, in fact, we know nothing at all. This, perhaps, cannot be proved; it is not easy to prove a negative; moreover, I do not propose to prove anything in this book; proof never convinces; but to say what is true in the right manner (if one could do it), that convinces. But whoever denies it, let him say what it is about his own child or wife that makes him love them while other children and women, equally dear to others, are indifferent to him. Thus we see that everything with which we come into direct contact is force; force acts on our senses; our active nature, by means of force, acts upon forces in the outer world. The intellectual nature, removed back from the outer world behind the outer sensory motor tract, deals with relations. The moral nature, still farther withdrawn into the inmost recesses of ourselves, whether considered physically or spiritually, deals with something still farther removed from force than are those relations which confront the intellect, and has to do with an unknown quantity which, for want of a better name, we call qualities. The relation of the intellect to these other two groups of reactive functions may, perhaps, be made clearer by a comparison which seems to me singularly exact. A sunbeam dispersed by a prism falls upon a screen; in the middle of the dispersed ray is a space of light; this represents the intellect; below the light are the heat rays, and above it the chemical rays. Let the heat rays represent the moral nature and the chemical rays the active nature, and the parallel between the solar ray and the whole reactive part of man is very complete. We have, then, three groups of existence in the outer world, and corresponding to them, three groups of functions in the inner world, the first being undoubtedly the *raison d'être* of the last, for without the preëxistence of the first we could not conceive the last coming into being.

For greater clearness the results of this chapter may be summed up in a tabular form as follows :—

Man. External World.
- Senses or Receptive Functions. Forces.
- Reactive Functions. Force, Phenomena, Qualities.
  - Active Nature. Forces, as Motion, Heat, and Light.
  - Intellectual Nature. Phenomena, and Relations of Coexistence and Sequence.
    - External or Receptive and Registering Functions, as Perception, Conception, and Memory. Concrete Sciences, as Botany, Zoölogy and Geology.
    - Internal or Reflective Functions, as Ratiocination, Comparison, and Judgment. Abstract Sciences, as Mathematics, Astronomy, Physics, Chemistry, Biology and Sociology.
  - Moral Nature. Qualities.
    - Positive Functions: Love and Faith. Beauty, Goodness.
    - Negative Functions: Hate and Fear. Ugliness, Evil.

CHAPTER II.

THE MORAL NATURE AND ITS LIMITS.

"If then, there is a philosophical discipline which examines into conditions of sensuous perception, and if there is a philosophical discipline which examines into the conditions of rational conception, there is clearly a place for a third philosophical discipline that has to examine into the conditions of that third faculty of man, coördinate with sense and reason —the faculty of perceiving the infinite which is at the root of all religions. . . . I know no better name for it than the faculty of faith."—MAX MÜLLER.

"Are you quite sure that those beliefs and dogmas are primary and not derived? that they are not the products instead of being the creators of man's moral nature?"—JOHN TYNDALL.

WHAT is the moral nature? and what are the lines between it and the active nature, between it and the intellectual nature, and between it and sense impressions? The moral nature is a bundle of faculties. Most of these faculties, though not all of them, are called passions and emotions. All passions and all emotions belong to, are part of, the moral nature, but the whole moral nature is not included in these two expressions. Love, faith, hate, fear, are the most prominent functions of the moral nature, if they are not, indeed, the whole of it. These are pure moral qualities; that is, each one of them is a distinct moral function, and, therefore, a simple moral function. The line between the active nature and the moral nature is not difficult to draw, though it is constantly overlooked. The active nature and the moral nature scarcely ever come in direct contact, the intellectual nature nearly always intervening between them. An act which is prompted by passion or emotion is directed by the intelligence; for instance, I desire something—I think how I shall obtain it—then go and get it; I hate some one—I think of some act that will injure him—then do it; I love some one—think what acts give pleasure to that person—then perform them. But people have a way of speaking of certain acts as being good—of other acts as being bad—of certain conduct as being moral—of certain other conduct as being immoral; is it the act, is it the conduct which is good, bad, moral, or immoral? It is not. No act or conduct can be good, bad, moral or immoral. Goodness, badness, morality and immorality belong solely to the moral nature. Acts are always outside the moral nature, and can have no moral quality. To kill a man is called an immoral act—a crime—but it is only called so because of the moral state which accompanies and prompts the act. Under many circumstances, homicide, although the act is precisely the same, has no moral significance; in certain circumstances of self-defense—in certain circumstances of mental alienation for example. Again, we know that the crime may be committed without the act—" Whosoever looketh on a woman to lust after her hath committed adultery with her already in his heart." To many these arguments will be unnecessary. Those who desire more illustrations of the position taken can easily think of as many as they choose for themselves. I shall take for granted that the line between the active nature and the moral nature is plain enough. But the line between the intellectual nature and the moral nature, though true and certain, is not quite so easy to draw or to see when it is drawn, for these two lie closer together than do the active nature and moral nature, and the functions of the intellectual nature are less easily defined, and are more like the functions of the moral nature than are those of the active nature. To the ordinary apprehension, however, I hope to make this line also sufficiently clear.

The intellect knows; the moral nature feels— that seems clear enough. Perception, conception, memory, reason, comparison, understanding, judgment, belong to, are parts of, the intellect. Love, hate, faith, fear, belong to, are functions of, the moral nature; that seems quite clear, and will probably be disputed by very few. But we all know that these two sets of functions are, in their manifestations, commonly blended together. That is to say, the idea of a thing or person having arisen in the mind, a feeling of pity, tenderness, love, hate, dislike, fear, annoyance, or a feeling of some kind arises at or about the same time, and is directed toward the same thing or person; and to all appearance the idea and the feeling arise together and are simply two aspects of one mental act. Now, what I wish to argue is that this is not the correct view to take of the matter at all; but that either the idea at first arises and then the feeling which may be said to color it, or that the feeling having arisen primarily, it either suggests the idea by association and then colors it; or the idea being suggested by something else besides the feeling, it is, all the same, colored by it, to a greater or less degree.

The essential distinctions of these two sets of functions is shown in the first place by the fact that a continuous current of ideational states and a continuous current of emotional states constantly exist, and flow on side by side without interfering with one another, except through association of certain ideas with certain emotional states. Any idea may exist at the same time as, and therefore be associated in consciousness with, almost any emotional state—that is to say, there is no fixedness of relation between ideas and emotional states. Any idea may exist without the coexistence of any emotional state. Any simple emotional state—faith, love, fear, or hate, may exist without being associated with any idea, that is, without the simultaneous existence of any thought. Moreover, there is no relation between the intensity of emotional and intellectual action going on at the same time; for, during states of strong emotional excitement the intellect may be very active or the reverse, and during periods of intense intellectual activity there may be either a great deal of emotional excitement or very little. And further, there is an absence of relation of development between the intellectual and moral nature which could hardly exist were these two not radically distinct from one another; for in any given individual the intellect may be highly developed and the moral nature very ill-developed, or the reverse; so that we often see clever men with bad hearts and men of excellent moral qualities who are very stupid. We all know instances of these two classes of men as well in actual life as in history. And passing from ordinary life downward to that life which is below the ordinary level of humanity, the lower level upon which the individual stands may be due to the deficiency of the intellectual or of the moral nature. For if the intellect is below the standard proper to ordinary man we say the man is a fool; if it is still further deficient we say he is an idiot. But if it is the moral nature which is deficient in development we say the man is a criminal, if not in act at least by nature; and if the moral nature is still further deficient we say the man is a moral idiot. But the fool may have a kind and affectionate heart and the criminal a quick wit. The intellectual idiot may still have the fundamental affections of our race fairly developed, and the moral idiot, though his intellect is not likely to be of a high order, may be a long way from a fool. It is undoubtedly true that there is a certain relation between intellectual and moral elevation and defect, so that they are apt to coexist, but this tendency is not greater than is the tendency of any two parts of an organism to be perfect or defective together in accordance with the more or less perfect impulses and conditions by which the life has been originated and is maintained.

To show the line between the intellectual nature and the moral nature, it will be necessary to discuss the nature of the relation—manifestly a very close one—which exists between them; and to get at this relation, it will be necessary to resolve in thought both the intellectual and moral natures as far as possible, by a process of mental analysis, into their ultimate elements. Now, the ultimate elements of the intellectual nature are concepts—that is, simple ideas; as, for instance, the idea of a color, a shape, a distance, a weight, or a sound; these concepts are formed by a process entirely unknown to us from the impressions made by external forces upon our senses. These impressions themselves, no doubt very different from our idea of them, are outside the mind, that is to say, unthinkable by us. These concepts are the elements of which the intellectual nature is built up; the getting of them we call conception; the combining, separating, and comparing of them, either as simple concepts or as already combined groups of concepts, we call reasoning, abstraction, imagination; the registering of the simple or compound concepts we call memory, and so on. Now, the simplest of these concepts that we can reach by our best efforts of analysis, such as the idea of time, space, or size, is undoubtedly an extremely complex thing, built up of elements which do not singly enter into consciousness, just as any piece of matter—a grain of sand, for instance—is an extremely complex thing, the ultimate atoms of which do not form objects of sense. The concepts in ordinary use, such as the idea of an author, a book, a dinner, or a holiday, one can see at a glance are infinitely more complex.

Let us now turn for a moment to the moral nature; this is much more simple than the intellectual nature, and by and by we shall see what appears to be the true anatomical explanation of this fact. The elements of the moral nature are moral states, most of them being what we call emotions. These moral states are simple and compound; but there is this remarkable difference between compound moral states and compound concepts, that whereas concepts can be compounded to almost any conceivable degree without the union of emotional states in the compound, moral states can hardly be compounded at all without combining them with concepts. A plausible anatomical reason for this will also appear later. The chief simple elements of the moral nature are love, faith, hate, and fear. A moment's reflection upon these four leading elements of the moral nature reveals to us <u>two</u> striking modes in which they differ from <u>concepts</u>. In the first place, they stand in pairs, the two elements of each pair—love, hate—faith, fear—being directly antithetic to each other. In the second place, they are all, by their nature, strongly contrasted to intellectual states by being continuous, while these last may be called, by contrast, instantaneous; this consideration will be more fully dwelt upon in another connection. I need scarcely say that it must be borne in mind that these moral states have all of them a wide range in degree. That, for instance, there is no difference in kind between a casual liking and the most intense love —between a slight feeling of dislike and the bitterest hate—between the faith that makes us take the word of an acquaintance for a few dollars, and the faith which enables the martyr to walk exultingly to the stake—between the feeling of uneasiness that something may be going wrong and the agony of extreme terror. And this capability of varying <u>in degree</u> forms a third strong line of demarkation between concepts and emotional states; for concepts, though they certainly stand out more strongly and clearly in the mind at some times than they do at others, yet have no such range of intensity as belongs to moral states. I do not pretend that I can say positively what moral states are simple and what are compound, or that I can analyze these last so as to show with certainty the elements of which they are composed. I venture the assertion, however, that the few moral states already mentioned, love, faith, hate, and fear, are simple. The grounds upon which I rest this assertion are that they are each of them capable of existing in the mind without the concurrent existence of any intellectual state, and that they defy analysis into simpler elements. These moral elements seem to me to differ in construction from concepts by being simpler than these last; for whereas, concepts analyzed to the last elements that the mind can reach, still seem, as mentioned above, aggregates of simple elements which the mind cannot grasp, moral elements show no sign of this composite formation, but seem to be absolutely homogeneous.

Are there any other simple moral states besides the four mentioned? I do not know. It will be safest in the present state of knowledge on the subject to rest content with these—to reduce what compound moral states we can into these and intellectual movements, and to leave the doubtful states alone.

The mind, then, is made up of simple moral

states and simple concepts, and of the infinite number of compounds which are formed from these. These compounds are of three kinds: 1. Compounds of simple moral states with one another; this class is very limited. 2. Compounds of concepts with one another. 3. Compounds of moral states and concepts. These two last classes are each of them practically infinite in extent, and make up between them almost the whole mind, including in that expression both the moral and intellectual natures. As in the formation of the earth's crust the simple chemical elements are few, and the compounds of them almost unlimited in number, so here; and as in examining the earth's crust we meet in rocks, soil, water, and living creatures, compounds of all degrees of complexity, but rarely a simple element, so here, in the world of mind, we scarcely ever meet with a simple element either moral or intellectual unless we obtain it by a process of analysis. But that simple elements must and do underlie and compose the compound crude products is as certain in the one case as it is in the other. In the case of the mind a very slight consideration serves to show that these simple elements are of two kinds, namely, moral states and intellectual concepts. Now, there are a few moral states which we can declare, with a high degree of probability, to be elementary and simple, and there are a large number which we can distinctly see to be composed of these and concepts. I do not say that this small number and this large number make up the whole moral nature, but at all events they make up enough of it to pass for all. Arguments which are based upon this large part are as stable as if based on the whole; and, indeed, my present impression is that the simple elements which I shall enumerate, and the compounds which they form with one another and with concepts, do make up the whole moral nature. These simple elements are four in number: they are, faith, love, fear, and hate. The test of the simplicity of these four moral states is, first, that they defy analysis; secondly, that they are any of them capable of existing in the mind alone, unassociated with any other moral state or with any concept; and thirdly, and as a consequence of the foregoing, the removal from the mind, either actually or in imagination, of any other element, whether intellectual or moral, is not necessarily followed by the removal of any one of these which may be present. Three of these terms, love, hate, and fear, do not require to be explained or defined; but the other, faith, stands in need of a few words of explanation. Faith is the opposite of fear as love is the opposite of hate. It is a purely moral function. It is strangely confounded in the popular mind with belief, which is a purely intellectual function. There is a connection between faith and belief which has led to this confusion, and this connection I will explain. Faith is defined by the author of the Epistle to the Hebrews as "the substance of things hoped for, the evidence of things not seen." This is an excellent definition, but requires to be itself explained. As I have said, faith is the opposite of fear, as love is the opposite of hate. Faith is almost synonymous with trust, confidence, and courage. My idea is that each of these words is used for faith in different intellectual connections. The best way to get an idea of what faith is, is to take a subject, such as our condition after death, or the character of the government of the universe as a whole in relation to ourselves—on neither of which subjects can our intellect throw any light —and study the attitude of our minds toward those subjects. Now, in knowledge, or rather want of knowledge, of either of these subjects, the savage and the civilized man are on equal terms, for they neither of them know anything about them at all; still, the mental attitude of the civilized man is very different from the mental attitude of the savage as toward these two subjects. If, then, the mental attitude is different, and if the intellectual nature has never dealt with these questions, as it certainly has not, then the difference must be due to a shifting of the moral attitude toward these subjects. And I think I can make it clear to any candid mind, upon a moderate amount of reflection, that this is what has actually happened in the course of man's upward march from savagery through barbarism to his present position which he calls civilization. Of course, I know that this is the direct reverse of what has always been imagined; it has been believed, and very naturally, that the shifting of the moral attitude was consequent upon a change in the intellectual attitude; whereas I say the change in the intellectual attitude is consequent upon a shifting of the moral attitude. As regards our condition after death, if our preponderant feeling, as it is in the case of the savage, be fear, we shall believe in a more or less inevitable state of suffering; if our preponderant feeling be faith, we shall believe in a more or less certain state of happiness in proportion to the development of this moral function. Many men, seeing that a fixed belief on such a subject, any knowledge of which is unattainable, is irrational, discard all belief, but they cannot discard their moral attitude, and this varies without a belief just as much and as little as with one. To show conclusively that the intellect has nothing to do with the state of feeling on this subject, it is only necessary to remark that the feeling is liable in many persons, if not in all, to a wide range of variation from time to time, the variations being governed by the state of the health and by other things, while the evidence, or rather want of evidence, and the belief on the subject remain fixed. Our mental attitude toward the government of the universe is decided in the same way by the degree of development of the moral nature, and especially by the degree of development of faith. The gods of savages are demons. The God of the better samples of Christians is a Being in whom goodness greatly preponderates over evil. The one believes as firmly in his god or gods as does the other, and one has as much and as little evidence upon which to base his belief as the other has. But one has less and the other has more faith. The character of the belief, therefore, is not in any degree determined by want of knowledge on the one hand, or by increased knowledge on the other, but solely by the amount of faith, of which the belief is simply an index. The belief itself is valueless in every sense. The faith which substitutes the higher belief for the lower is the most valuable of all our possessions. It is through this association that belief came to be considered so important; since men, having a certain grade of faith associated with a certain belief, easily fell into the error that the belief was the cause of the faith, was necessary to it, was even the faith itself; though a greater error than this, and, in its effects, a more injurious one to humanity, could scarcely be imagined. It is evident, to whoever will think of it, that with different persons, or with the same person at different times, the degree of faith may and does vary greatly with the same belief. So, the same degree of faith may and does coexist with a wide range of belief. This being so, it is plain that the belief of any given person only indicates the amount of his faith in a very broad and general sense; and the significance of what is called religious belief consists in this, that it is a test, and though a rough one, still the only test which we are capable of applying, to measure the faith of any given man or class of men. For a long time after the foundation of Christianity, for example, all faith, speaking generally, which was not associated in thought with the Christian belief, was lower than that which was interpreted in terms of the intellect by this belief; therefore, not to hold the Christian belief was a true mark of inferiority. This test is still applied, and this feeling still remains, and is likely to remain, in millions of minds for a long time yet, though the proposition upon which it rests is no longer true; for in the front ranks of humanity at present, and on an average, the Christian belief represents a lower phase of faith than exists in the minds of those who reject this doctrine.

Let us pass now to compound moral states and attempt to resolve some of them into simple moral states and concepts; that is, let us see which of them can be shown to be composed of the four simple moral elements, faith, love, hate, and fear, with or without the union of one or more concepts. Joy, high spirits, exultation, enthusiasm, and triumph are love and faith in their original non-differentiated form, generally, though by no means necessarily, combined with a more or less compound concept. And here I wish to say that, in a very low form of the moral nature, as it is seen in young children, and in all animals except the very highest, the two positive elements, love and faith, seem to be not yet separated, but to exist as one primitive function, and it is probable that, if we could go far enough back in the process of development, we should find the two negative elements, hate and fear, also merged into one primary form. In the course of development the original negative element is in advance of the original positive element, and in it separation occurred soonest. In young children, before love and faith make their appearance as separate functions, they may be observed existing in this primitive, non-differentiated form, and in this state we call them high spirits or joy. In the course of development of the individual man, after the division of the primitive positive element has become fully established, and love and faith have come into existence as two separate well-defined functions, the primitive, non-differentiated form still makes its appearance at times; but the separate elements into which it has divided, and their compounds, are by far more common than is this archaic form. Envy is hate combined with a certain very compound concept. Anger and hate are the same thing; there is no difference between hating a man and being angry with him; or, if there is a difference, it is simply that anger is a more transitory and less intense form of the same passion. The word jealousy is probably used, as nearly all words are which express compound emotional states, in several senses by different people, and perhaps by the same people at different times. Sometimes it is simply hate combined with a very complex concept. At other times it is composed of the two moral states, love and fear, combined with a very compound intellectual state. And this last is probably the condition to which the word most properly belongs. Grief is usually considered to be a simple emotional state, but this it certainly is not, because in the first place it cannot exist without the concurrent existence of a concept which enters into and makes part of it, and, in the second place, it cannot exist without the moral state, love, which also enters into and forms part of it. Now, no moral state can be called simple that requires for its existence another moral state or a concept. A mother loses her child by death, and her grief is intense; but if you could destroy in her heart love for the child her grief would cease at once. Grief, then, in this case, is love combined with a certain concept—death—but combined with this concept, and underneath it and concealed by it, is another moral state. Now, what moral state has been, both in man and animals, since the beginning of the world, combined with the concept death? You know that the moral state I allude to is fear. Grief, then, in the case supposed, is love combined with the concept, death, which concept is combined with the moral state, fear. This analysis is hard to follow, because the associations in this compound have existed so long that the union has become what we may call organized; still, I know that this, or something very like it, is the true composition of grief. The analysis is easier to follow and realize if we suppose that the child is not dead but dying; here you can detect plainly love and the fear of death constituting the passion, grief. Now, is it not plain why the analysis is easier to make in the last case than in the first? The reason is, that grief in the case of actual death existed in the minds of our ancestors for millions of years before they became intelligent enough to grieve for imminent death, and also because the association of fear with the concept, death, existed in their minds for perhaps millions of generations before the compound which we call grief came into existence. The constituents of grief, then, in the case of the dying child, have not had time to become organized into an apparently simple passion to anything like the same degree as in the case of the dead child.

The opposites of joy, high spirits, exultation, enthusiasm, and triumph, which are compounds of love and faith, or rather which are these two moral functions in their archaic, non-differentiated form, are sadness, low spirits, depression, dejection, and despair. These are compounds of hate and fear in varying degrees of intensity, and in varying proportions, and combined or not with concepts. Hope is a compound of love and faith with a concept. It is not love and faith in their undivided archaic form, but the two separate functions combined with a concept. Repentance is, in the same way, a compound of hate and fear —hate of an act committed, and fear of the consequences. Let the hate be reduced and the fear increased, and the repentance becomes remorse. Let the hate be reduced to a minimum and the fear increased to a maximum, and the feeling is despair. These are <u>all immoral states,</u> as will be seen farther on, s<u>ince they are made up of the negative moral functions</u>. Among the compounds of faith and hate are pride, the combative passions, and probably others; but these analyses have now been carried far enough for our present purpose.

The analyses given are of the most simple of ordinary mental states. They are, doubtless, very incomplete, and probably some of them very incorrect. Most ordinary mental states are made up of compounds of compounds of simple states, and even of compounds of compounds of compounds, and defy even such imperfect analysis as the above. There are no compounds of love and hate or of faith and fear, because these, being the opposites of one another, in the sense that heat and cold are opposites, are mutually exclusive the one of the other. The compound emotions are always on this view:—1. Compounds of love and faith. 2. Compounds of hate and fear. 3. Compounds of love and fear. 4. Compounds of faith and hate. But each of these compounds constitutes a large class—the variety in the individual compound states being due, in the first place, to variation in the proportion of the two moral constituents, and, in the second place, to the union of the compound moral state with a wide range of concepts. Does it appear strange that the immense variety of human passion, sentiment, and emotion could be produced by the combination of so few simple elements? If it does, consider the compounds of carbon and hydrogen, their enormous number and great dissimilarity, and I think that the strangeness will disappear.

Concepts and emotional states being the elements by means of whose union the mind is built up, let us see, if we can, what laws govern their association. In the first place it is clear that the union of simple concepts is more elementary and stronger than the union of any concept with any emotional state, and that, as said above, the union of these ideational elements can be carried to any extent of which our minds are capable just as well without as with the presence of emotional states. In the second place, there is no true union of two emotional states forming thus a compound emotional state without the presence of an idea, except in the case of love and faith and of hate and fear, which cases are exceptional, since each of these pairs seems to have sprung from an archaic form which contained potentially the two functions. That, in other words, although a simple emotion may and often does exist in the mind unassociated with any idea, a compound emotion, except as above, cannot so exist. The third law is found in chemistry as well as in psychology. It is, that binary combinations of concepts are more stable than tertiary combinations, and these than more complex combinations of concepts; and that binary combinations of a concept and a simple emotional state are more stable than tertiary combinations of these elements, and these than still more complex combinations. Simple concepts being probably few in number and accessible to all, the complexity and fineness of the adhesions between them constitute largely the value of a given intellect. The union of ideas with emotional states makes up character. Our feeling toward individuals of our race, as well those related to us or known to us as those whom we casually meet; our feeling to the race at large, to animals, to external nature, to the unknowable which surrounds us upon all sides, to ourselves, to death, and, in fact, the adhesion or want of adhesion between all ideas and all moral states, is what we call character in its infinite variety. With some people the adhesions between moral states and concepts are such as are justified by the opinions and expediencies of the societies in which they live, and such people are said to be good people. With others, with equally good moral natures, the adhesions are not such as the opinion of the time and place justifies, and they are said to be bad people. It will be seen, therefore, that to have a high moral nature and to be a good man are not synonymous terms. It will be remembered by all that many men with the highest moral natures have been put to death as bad men, the reason being that the adhesions and want of adhesions in their minds between moral states and concepts were such as current opinion could not tolerate. Given two men in whom the associations between their moral states and concepts are the same, and the man with the highest moral nature will be admitted by all to be the better man. Given two men with equally high moral natures, and it is plain he will be called the better man of the two in whom the intellectual and moral associations are most similar to those of his contemporaries. Again, with some people these bonds are exceptionally loose, and we say that such an one is unstable, or is weak, or that he has a weak character; with another the bonds are exceptionally firm, and we say that such a person is obstinate, or that such an one possesses great firmness of character.

The value and character of a given mind is therefore determined by the absolute and relative development of the different functions of the moral nature; by the absolute and relative development of the different functions of the intellectual nature; and especially by the associations formed in the past of the individual, or transmitted to him by his ancestors, between the moral states and concepts of which his mind is composed; and lastly, by the firmness of these adhesions.

The fear of death and maternal love are two

good examples of associations of this kind. These exist not only throughout the whole human family, but have a foremost place in the psychical life of all sentient creatures. No one will deny that a strong bond of association exists between the emotion fear and the thought of self death; for the thought of death, apart from self death, is not by any means so intimately connected with this emotion; and when we actually lose by death those whom we most love, we grieve for our loss, not because a great misfortune has befallen them. The intimate association between this emotion and this mental image is shown by the fact that if the emotion fear be primarily strongly excited, as in such pathological conditions as will be referred to in the next chapter, the almost inevitable consequence is that the thought of self death arises at once in the mind, though the bodily health may be at the time tolerably good, and the person no more likely to die then than at any other period of his or her life. On the other hand, in a state of health, let self death appear to the reason to be imminent, and with most people the emotion fear is felt in a lively manner within a very short time thereafter. Now, why is this? Why does the emotion fear excite the idea of death, and why does the idea of death excite the emotion fear? It is not because we know death to be an evil, for we know nothing about it; and even if we knew it to be, past all doubt, a very great evil, that would not explain such an association as exists. For, other things which we have every reason to believe to be the greatest evils, such as sin, poverty, and disease, have not—that is, the thought of them has not—the same intimate relation with the emotion fear. Neither is it because we fear the pain which often accompanies death, for if we had every reason to be sure that the death would be painless the fear would equally exist. Besides, when men actually come to die, either by some disease which leaves the mind intact, or by an execution, they have little or no fear. As soon as death is certain, inevitable, close, the Dweller on the Threshold departs and leaves the door between the known and unknown open and the passage unobstructed.

The fact is that the association between fear and the thought of self death has no basis, so far as we know, or have reason to think, in the truth of things, but is purely artificial, and is, beyond question, the result of natural selection operating upon countless generations. For, given a race, either of men or of inferior animals, in whom this association did not exist, and the life of that race, in such a world as this, where every species is surrounded and permeated by causes of destruction, would be a short one. But, given a race or a family of races, emerging from unconscious into conscious existence, and through countless ages rising to higher and higher phases of life, and it is easy to see that, other things being equal, the individuals in whom this association began to exist, ever so faintly, would often live where their neighbors would die. They would transmit the association to their offspring, among whom the individuals in whom this psychical feature was more marked would have an advantage over those in whom it was less marked; and so the tendency would be for the association to grow stronger and stronger until a point was reached in the history of development at which, on the one hand, reason began to protest against the closeness of this alliance, and, on the other hand, the family affections and the sense of duty and religion began to take the place of crude fear, and to make this association less necessary. The mastery of the higher emotions over the initial union is shown by the readiness with which men of the higher races face death in pursuance of what they consider to be a good cause, such as the cause of religion or national honor. If this reasoning be true—and it is true—then here, in the deepest part of our nature, circumstances have compelled humanity, through countless ages, to affirm a lie. In the case of our own ancestors, the culminating point of this association was reached and passed before the separation of the Arian people on the plains of Central Asia—before the existence of the distinct races who spoke Sanscrit, Greek, and Latin. And we can only judge now what the strength of this union was then by the observation of races whose present stage of development is on a par with our condition at that time. And we know, from the universal testimony of travelers, and many of us from our own observation, that fear bears a much larger proportion to the other emotions in the savage mind than in the civilized—that it is even absolutely more developed; and that its union with the idea of death is stronger in them than it is in civilized man.

The union existing between love in the bosom of the mother and the mental image of her child is as strong as, if not stronger than, any other association of a moral state with an idea. So strong is this association that almost all kindly feeling not only in the grown-up woman but in the female child as well suggests this mental image in some form or other. In the child it takes the form of a doll. To the childless woman a dog, or perhaps a cat, supplies the place of the infant which should exist but does not. On the other hand, the mental image of all forms of helplessness and infancy awaken in the female mind this motherly tenderness. This union is, no doubt, largely due, as in the case last considered, to the influence of

— natural selection, since this cohesion is as needful to the continuance of the life of the race as the other cohesion is to the continuance of the life of the individual. Why not, therefore, say of this as of the other association that it is a fraud perpetrated by circumstances? Why not say that this association, also, is purely artificial, and has no warrant in the truth of things? This book is intended as an answer to this question; I cannot pause to discuss it in this chapter. I may say here, however, that the question really is:—Does the central fact of the universe, as it stands related to us, justify on our part fear and hate, or love and faith, or does it justify neither? I believe, and I believe I shall show before I finish this book, that it justifies love and faith. The associations are, both of them, undoubtedly, the fortuitous products of circumstances. But if love and faith are justified, and fear and hate are not, then it is certain that maternal love is justified, and that fear of death is not justified.

In the development of a race the formation of these bonds, almost infinite in number, and requiring to have a definite relative strength, within certain limits of variation, is of at least as great importance as the actual development of either the moral or intellectual natures. And derangement of these associations, the loosening of some which are essential to life in a social state, and the formation *de novo*, or the increased intimacy of union of others which are trivial, valueless, mischievous—I say such derangements of associations between moral states and intellectual concepts, and going deeper, derangements of the union of intellectual concepts with one another, constitute the characteristic mental lesion in many cases of insanity, and such derangements probably constitute a material part of all insanity.

Our actual mental life, then, consists in a constant succession of these two sets of elements, elaborately and more or less intimately combined, and if I have failed to make clear the fine line which separates them, the next chapter, in which I shall try to determine the anatomical seat of the moral nature, will assist materially in making this line clearer; and it will be seen that I have placed in that chapter a number of arguments which belong as much to this chapter as they do to that—such as the depth of the moral nature, the rhythmic character of its functions, their continuity, their range of intensity, and their simplicity as compared with concepts. If I have made clear the lines of separation between the moral nature and the active nature, and between the moral nature and the intellectual nature, it only remains to draw the line distinctly between the moral nature and sense impressions, and the moral nature will be isolated and will stand out by itself separated from all other parts of conscious life. I know I have not made the lines already drawn very plain, and I do not hope to make the line which remains to be drawn any plainer. I trust, however, that the honest and intelligent reader will see with reasonable clearness what is intended, and that his intellect will make up for what is lacking in mine. Sense impressions and emotional states are often so far apart, that looking upon these examples of them they do not seem likely to be confused; thus the touch and sight of this book are as distinct from love or fear as one thing can well be from another. At other times the sense impression and the moral state actually touch—even run together. In listening to music certain moral states are produced. Where, in this case, does the sense impression end and the moral state begin? All that part of the total sensori-emotional condition which can be re-excited without the sound of music, as by thinking over or reading the score, belongs to the moral nature; all the rest belongs to sense. But this statement is liable to be misunderstood. If it were taken literally and boldly it might be said: Well, then, the sense impression is far the most important part of the music, for no one can derive half the pleasure from thinking over or reading the score that he derives from hearing the music well executed. The answer to this is that it is not supposed that the emotional state—though the same, and covering the same ground—will be nearly so intensely excited by the reading as by the hearing. Take this element into consideration, and the definition will be complete enough. This test is capable of being applied to every case where sense impressions and moral states come in contact; and by it the line between these may always be drawn nearly enough for the purposes of this essay. Another way to set forth the line between the senses and the moral nature would be to say that pleasure and pain belong to the former, and happiness and unhappiness to the latter, for love and faith are the elements of happiness, and hate and fear the elements of unhappiness; that, consequently, a person may be happy while suffering pain, and unhappy in the midst of pleasure. And there is no harm in pleasure in itself, whatever moralists may have said, but those who depend on pleasure for the enjoyment of life are very apt to neglect the cultivation of the elements of happiness; and often not only neglect them, but interpose the most serious obstacles to their development. When this happens pleasure becomes immoral and at the same time impolitic. On the other hand, there is no doubt that the gratification of the senses in moderation stimulates the development of the positive moral functions, *i. e.*, love and faith, and that to refuse the senses their due gratification is just as immoral and impolitic as it is to abandon oneself to a sensual life.

CHAPTER III.

THE PHYSICAL BASIS OF THE MORAL NATURE.

"Tout ce qui est relatif aux passions appartient à la vie organique. . . . Concluons donc de ces diverses considérations, que c'est toujours sur la vie organique, et non sur la vie animale que les passions portent leur influence. . . . Tout tend donc à prouver que la vie organique est le terme où aboutissent, et le centre d'où portent, les passions."—BICHAT.

"The organic nervous centres are the centres also of those mental acts which are not volitional, but are instinctive, impulsive, or, as they are most commonly called, emotional."—RICHARDSON.

I HAVE said, in a former chapter, that the physical basis of the moral nature is probably the great sympathetic nervous system. Let us see what arguments can be found to support this view. To reach these arguments it will be necessary to consider the whole subject of the functions of the great sympathetic, and to do this we must dwell for a few moments upon the structure of this vast and complicated organ.

The great sympathetic consists, in the first place, of a double chain of ganglia, over fifty in number, extending from the base of the brain along the sides of the spinal column to the coccyx; in the second place, of certain ganglia, such as the superficial and deep cardiac, the semilunar, and innumerable others, named and unnamed, scattered among the thoracic, abdominal, and pelvic viscera ; and, in the third place, of an almost infinite number of nerve cords which may be divided into three classes: first, those which connect the sympathetic ganglia to one another (many of these are not, strictly speaking, nerve cords, though cord-like in form, but are prolongations of the ganglia, and are made up not of nerve fibres but of nerve cells); next, those which connect the sympathetic ganglia with the nerve trunks and the nerve centres of the cerebro-spinal nervous system; and lastly, those which take their origin in the ganglia of the great sympathetic nervous system, and are distributed to the various organs which are supplied with nerves from this nervous system.

It must not be supposed that this brief *résumé* gives any adequate idea of the extent of the distribution or the amount of the aggregate mass of the great sympathetic. No part of the body is entirely without sympathetic fibres, and the ganglia of this system are almost as universally distributed as are its nerve cords, so that the whole mass of the great sympathetic, though it cannot be determined with anything approaching to accuracy, must be very much greater than is often supposed, and perhaps does not fall much short of the mass of the cerebro-spinal nervous system. Indeed, one author (Davy) goes so far as to say that it "constitutes a great part of the volume and weight of the whole body."

In minute structure the great sympathetic is composed, like the cerebro-spinal nervous system, of cells and fibres. Neither its cells nor its fibres, however, are like those belonging to the brain

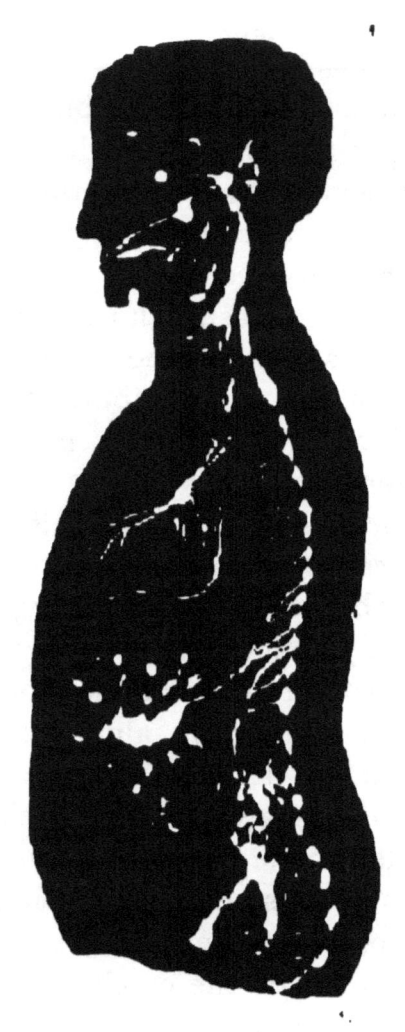

and cord. There is enough difference in minute anatomy between these two systems to make a thoughtful observer feel certain that there must be a decided difference in their functions.

The only other thing to be especially remarked about the anatomy of this great nerve is the immense number and great complexity of its plexuses. These plexuses, speaking generally, are made up of nerve cords from different sympathetic ganglia, of filaments derived from spinal nerves, and often others from cranial nerves. That is, in a given plexus there will unite nerves from, perhaps, two, three, or more sympathetic ganglia, with filaments from one or more spinal nerves, and, perhaps, from one or two cranial nerves. From these plexuses the nerve cords proceed to their ultimate distribution, the object of the plexus seeming to be to bring together and combine these various elements in order to form an extremely complex nerve.

Now, as regards the ultimate distribution of the great sympathetic—a matter of great importance in deciding upon its functions. In the first place, it sends branches to all the spinal and cranial nerves, which presumably follow the course of those nerves, and are distributed with them to the organs supplied with nerves by the cerebrospinal nervous system. Secondly, it is distributed to the coats of all the arteries in the body, though the arteries carrying blood to the head, face, and glandular organs are better supplied by it than others. Thus, the common, internal, and external carotids, the phrenic, the renal, the hepatic, the splenic, the superior mesenteric, sacral, internal iliac, vesical, and uterine arteries are known to be freely supplied by it. Thirdly, the viscera—thoracic, abdominal, and pelvic—are all supplied more or less abundantly with sympathetic nerves.

I will mention some of the different organs in their order, according to the amount of the supply relative to their mass which they severally receive, as well as I have been able to make it out; but I must state that this classification is only approximative—of two such organs, for instance, as the spleen and pancreas, it is impossible to say which is the better supplied. It will be seen as we go on that this classification, although imperfect, is somewhat important in view of the deductions which we shall be able to draw from it.

At the head of the list, beyond all question, stands the heart; for it not only receives the six cardiac nerves from the upper, middle, and inferior cervical ganglia, and has four plexuses—the two cardiac and two coronary—entirely devoted to its supply, but it has also numerous ganglia imbedded in its substance, which are centres of nerve force for its own use, over and above. Next to the heart come the suprarenal capsules.

In the third rank stand, I think, the sexual organs, both male and female, the testes and ovaries being especially well supplied. The organs of special sense come next—the eye, the internal ear, the nasal mucous membrane, and the palate. Next after these organs must be placed the stomach, the whole intestinal tract, and the liver. In the sixth rank stand the thyroid gland, kidneys, spleen, and pancreas. Then come the lungs, which receive in proportion to their size a remarkably small supply.

There is just one thing more to say about the anatomy of our subject before proceeding to its physiology, and that is, to indicate a list of organs supplied by the sympathetic and not by the cerebro-spinal nervous system. And it is well to bear in mind that this division of parts is not absolute but relative; for as the sympathetic, in all its extent, probably has cerebro-spinal fibres mixed with it, so all parts which are supplied with nerves by it no doubt do receive some filaments from the cerebro-spinal nervous system; but these fibres are small and few, and are probably also modified in their functions by being so intimately associated as they are with sympathetic nerves and ganglia. The division of organs, therefore, into those supplied by both systems, and those supplied by the sympathetic alone, though not an absolute division, is still a real one. In this list we have the radiating fibres of the iris, the arterial coats, the liver, the kidneys, the ovaries, the suprarenal capsules, the pancreas, and the intestinal tract including both muscular coat and glands, and to this list, I believe, may be fairly added the body of the bladder and that of the uterus.

Now, as to the functions of the great sympathetic. Most physiologists seem to consider that the sympathetic differs very little in its functions from the cerebro-spinal system, and that, at least in some respects, its functions are identical with the functions of this latter nervous system. There are some general considerations which make this view of the subject appear to me unlikely to be correct. In the first place, though both nervous systems are made up of nerve cells and nerve fibres, yet the cells and fibres of the great sympathetic nervous system differ materially in structure from the cells and fibres of the cerebro-spinal nervous system, and it can scarcely be supposed that such difference in structure should not be manifested by some corresponding difference in function. In the second place, the great sympathetic system, in the arrangement of its parts, in the great number and extraordinary diffusion of its ganglia, and in the immense number and great complexity of its plexuses, is too unlike the cerebro-spinal nervous system for us to suppose that their functions can be anything like identical. Thirdly, the great sympathetic is distributed mainly to organs in the interior of the body that do not require and are not endowed with sensibility—at all events to anything like the same degree as obtains in the case of the external organs which are supplied with nerves by the cerebro-spinal nervous system. And lastly, if the great sympathetic has the power of exciting contractility in muscles at all, we shall see that this power is materially different from that possessed by the motor centres of the cerebro-spinal system.

What, then, are the functions of the sympathetic nervous system?

I shall consider this subject by seeking to give rational answers, deduced from acknowledged facts, to the following five questions:

First: Is it a motor nervous system; and if so, in what sense?

Second: Is it endowed with sensation?

Third: Does it control the functions of the secreting glands, as the gastric, mammary, intestinal, salivary, lachrymal, the liver, kidneys, and pancreas?

Fourth: Does it influence the general nutrition of the body; and if so, in what manner?

Fifth: Is it the nervous centre of the moral nature?

Let us discuss these questions in their order.

I. The first question is: Does the sympathetic possess the functions of a motor nerve? The only muscular structures which receive nerves from the sympathetic and none from the cerebro-spinal nervous system are the muscular coats of the arteries, the radiating fibres of the iris, and the muscular coat of the intestines. It would be almost though not absolutely correct to include in this list the bladder and uterus. Any nervous stimulation received by these organs must, therefore, be sent from the great sympathetic, and that these structures are influenced by some nervous system is certain, as we shall see farther on. We may, therefore, say positively that the great sympathetic does act as a nerve of motion. It is to be remarked, however, that all these structures are made up of unstriped muscular fibre; and also that all unstriped muscle, whether it receive any nerves from the cerebro-spinal nervous system or not, is well supplied by the great sympathetic. We shall be safe if we infer from these facts that the great sympathetic is the nerve of motion to unstriped muscle. In the case of the heart, whose muscular fibres are striped, though they are not precisely similar to ordinary striped muscle such as is supplied by the cerebro-spinal system and is under the control of the will, there seems no room to doubt that its movements are influenced by the great sympathetic. And this must be taken as a partial exception to what I believe to be the law, namely: that the movements of striped muscle are controlled by the cerebro-spinal nervous system, and the movements of unstriped muscle by the great sympathetic. The only other exception to this law that I am aware of is the case of the circular fibres of the iris, which, being unstriped muscle, are supplied by the third cranial nerve.

II. If the same reasoning be applied to the solution of the question: Is the great sympathetic a sensory nerve? we do not get a very clear answer. Parts supplied only by the great sympathetic, as the liver, kidneys, pancreas, suprarenal capsules, and ovaries, are probably very little if at all sensitive. Arguments as to the sensitiveness of these organs drawn from pathological conditions I do not think of much value, for such pathological states usually involve the investing membrane of these organs either by congestion of it, stretching of it, or in some other way, and it is known that this investing membrane, the peritoneum, is well supplied by cerebro-spinal nerves, and is very sensitive. On the other hand, pathological conditions of these organs which do not interfere with their investing membrane—such as cancer of the liver, in cases where all the cancerous nodules are buried in the substance of the organ and do not encroach upon the peritoneum—and many diseases, both of the liver and kidneys, leading to fatal disintegration of tissue, are quite painless. The organs which have been mentioned as being supplied solely by great sympathetic nerves are, by their position, well protected, both by being surrounded by sensitive tissues and organs, and by being invested by a highly sensitive membrane. They do not, therefore, require for their protection that they themselves should be sensitive, and I do not believe that they are so. Another fact which bears out this view remains to be mentioned. When organs analogous to those of which we have been speaking—that is, other glands, such as the mammary, salivary, or testes —are placed in exposed situations, they are then supplied with cerebro-spinal nerves as well as with nerves from the sympathetic; the sympathetic fibres being undoubtedly intended to control their functions, and the cerebro-spinal fibres to make them sensitive and so protect them from injury. For if, on the one hand, the great sympathetic fibres were endowed with sensibility, there would be no occasion for a supply of cerebro-spinal nerves to these organs; or if, on the other hand, the cerebro-spinal nerves are not sent to furnish them with sensibility, but to control, as some physiologists maintain, their secreting functions, then there would be no apparent reason why they should be supplied with great sympathetic nerves. All things considered, therefore, I am inclined to answer this question in the negative. I do not believe that the great sympathetic is endowed with sensation. Of course I do not mean that the great sympathetic has not afferent as well as efferent fibres—it doubtless has; but what I argue is, that an afferent impulse along these fibres, although it may and does awake a response in the corresponding ganglion, does not awaken sensation.

III. The third question is: Does the great sympathetic exercise a controlling influence over the functions of the secreting glands? I think there need be no hesitation about answering this question in the affirmative. The ordinary functions of these glands might be supposed to be carried on independently of nervous influence altogether, although I do not think it at all likely that they are; for, as in the healthy condition of the body the secreting process of every gland is carried on with reference to other parts besides itself, so there seems no means by which the function of a given gland could be coördinated to the condition of other parts of the economy except through the agency of a nervous system distributed to each, and through which a chain of intelligence —if we may use that word—is maintained. If any nervous system performs the office here indicated, it must, of necessity, be the great sympathetic, for the following reasons :—The will has no influence upon the functions of the secreting glands. In cases of general paralysis from disease or injury of the cord the functions of the secreting glands are performed almost if not quite as well as when the cerebro-spinal system is intact. The great sympathetic is the only nervous system which is distributed to all the glands, the liver and kidneys receiving nerves from no other.

As for the cases of extraordinary action, or arrest of action, of these glands in some emotional states, as, for example, the excessive secretion of urine in fear, of tears in grief, and conversely, the arrest of the buccal and salivary secretions in terror, the arrest of the gastric secretion from almost any marked emotional excitement, the well-known increase, arrest, and alteration in quality of the mammary secretion from the influence of maternal love, terror, and rage ; these cannot be explained without referring them to the influence of some nervous system over the glands in question. I think, for the following reasons, that this nervous system is the sympathetic :—In the first place, some of these glands, as the kidneys, receive no other than sympathetic nerves ; and, in the second place, the great sympathetic sends a liberal supply of nerves to all of them. It sends nerves to those glands which receive cerebro-spinal nerves, as well as to those which do not; and if reference be made to an attempted classification on a previous page of this book, it will be seen that there the kidneys, which receive no nerves but from the great sympathetic, rank in the sixth order of organs according to the quantity of sympathetic nerves which they receive. The testes, ovaries, the gastric and intestinal glands, all come before the kidneys as receiving more sympathetic nerves than do these. Of these organs the ovaries, suprarenal capsules, and liver receive no cerebro-spinal nerves, but the other organs all do, and some of them, as the testes and gastric glands, receive a tolerably large supply of nerves from this system. If, then, some secreting organs are certainly influenced by emotional states through the medium of the sympathetic, and if the great sympathetic is supplied just as copiously, or more so, to other organs whose functions are also influenced by emotional states, is it not reasonable to conclude that the medium is the same in all cases, and that it is through the great sympathetic that emotional conditions affect the secretions?

But this is not all. We have seen above that it is a strict rule that secreting glands are supplied with cerebro-spinal nerves copiously, or the reverse, according to the degree of their exposure to injury from without; thus the salivary and mammary glands are well supplied, while the kidneys and liver receive no cerebro-spinal fibres at all. So too, the testes are supplied with cerebro-spinal nerves, while the homologous organs in the female—the ovaries—are not. So that, on the one hand, without supposing that the cerebro-spinal nerves going to these organs have anything to do with their functions, we can understand why they are sent to them; and, on the other hand, we have shown that they are not needed to explain the functional phenomena of these organs, for these are the same in glands which are, and in those which are not, supplied with cerebro-spinal fibres.

But there is still another word to say in support of this view, and it is this—cerebro-spinal nerves are either nerves of sensation or nerves of motion. Now, in the case, for instance, of the mammary glands, which are supplied with cerebro-spinal nerves derived from the anterior and lateral cutaneous nerves of the thorax, those branches which are distributed to the mammary glands are either sensory or motor nerves. Now, if we suppose that these nerves control the secreting functions of the glands, we must either suppose that a motor nerve is able to take on this function, which does not seem likely, or we must suppose that it is accomplished by a sensory nerve; and in that case we must argue that the nerves in question are capable

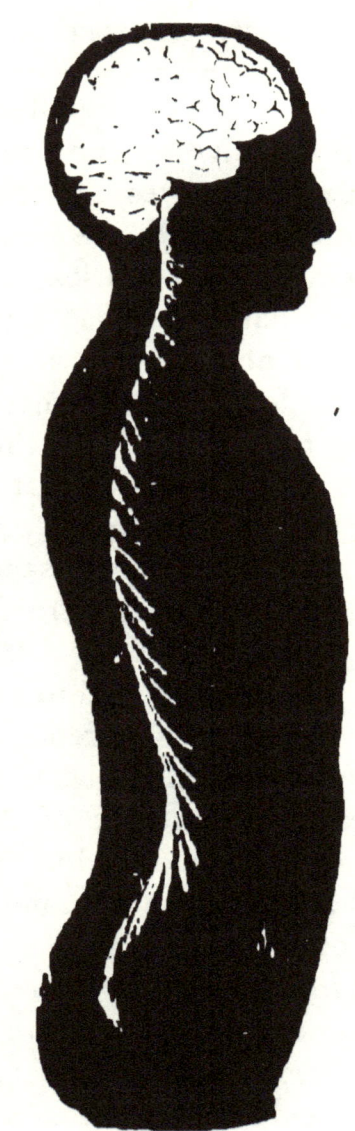

of carrying the current which has this influence on the gland the reverse way to its ordinary use, for the current in a sensory nerve flows from the periphery to the centre, but this current of nervous influence, of which there is now question, flows along the nerve from the centre to the periphery.

If these considerations are carefully weighed they will be seen to bear out the following propositions: That the great sympathetic can and does exercise a controlling influence over the functions of some of the secreting glands, such as the kidneys, which receive no other nerves. That, as it is at least equally distributed to other glands which receive cerebro-spinal nerves, and no other function appears for it to perform, it influences their secreting functions also. That cerebro-spinal nerves when sent to glands have another obvious function to perform besides that of controlling the secretions of these glands; and that it is, consequently, unnecessary to suppose that they perform this function also. And, finally, it does not seem likely, for other reasons, that the nerves derived from the cerebro-spinal system can or do influence the functions of secreting organs.

IV. The fourth question is: Does the great sympathetic influence the general nutrition of the body; and if so, in what manner? The nervous power which controls nutrition must be universal, since nutrition itself is universal. The great sympathetic nerve is distributed to the whole system, while many parts are not supplied by the cerebro-spinal system. For all cranial and spinal nerves receive branches from the sympathetic which are undoubtedly distributed, at least in part, with the spinal and cranial nerves. Also, all arteries are accompanied by sympathetic nerves which are distributed to the same parts as the arteries. Besides this there are, without any doubt, as pointed out by Davy, in his work on the great sympathetic, hundreds of minute sympathetic ganglia scattered among the tissues and organs of the body which send filaments to the parts in the neighborhood of each of them, so that, in fact, the distribution of the great sympathetic system is absolutely universal, while the distribution of the cerebro-spinal system is far from being so. The nutrition of paralyzed limbs, though not up to par on account of want of exercise, is still pretty well kept up; while if those limbs could be deprived of sympathetic nervous influence instead of cerebro-spinal nervous influence there is reason to believe that their nutrition would fail absolutely, and that they would die.

If the sympathetic be divided on one side of the neck, the immediate effects of the operation are as follows: The corresponding side of the head and face is immediately very much congested, and the temperature of the same parts rises as much as six, eight, or ten degrees. The meaning of these changes would seem to be that the muscular coats of the arteries are paralyzed by division of the nerve which supplies them, and that oxidation of the tissues takes place too rapidly. Whether oxidation of the tissues is hastened in consequence of the congestion which is due to the paralysis of the muscular coats of the arteries, or whether it is due to a direct loss of nervous energy supplied by the sympathetic to the tissues themselves, and by virtue of which retrograde metamorphosis is, in the normal state of the parts, held in check, or what part of the extra oxidation and consequent elevation of temperature is due to each of these causes, cannot, perhaps, be absolutely determined in the present state of our knowledge. It is in any case undoubtedly true that, either directly or indirectly, the great sympathetic exercises a controlling influence over that process of cell growth and destruction which we call nutrition. To what extent the process of nutrition is dependent upon a supply of nerve force derived from the sympathetic is a more difficult matter to decide. We know that this process goes on in plants, and in animals too low in the scale to have a sympathetic system, though Davy believes that all animals have a sympathetic system, and that even plants have an analogous organ ; but, supposing that the ordinary view is correct, and that neither plants nor animals very low in the scale have a sympathetic system, then it would seem that the process of nutrition cannot be entirely dependent upon any kind of nervous influence. But in that case it would appear that, while going on under the general laws of chemico-vital selection and of cell growth and destruction which are common to all organized beings, the highest as well as the lowest, to plants as well as to animals, nutrition is still subject to what we may call a general supervision of the great sympathetic system.

V. The last question which we have to answer in regard to the functions of the great sympathetic, is: Is it the nervous centre of the moral nature? I believe it is.

It has been pointed out in the previous chapter that there are several reasons for supposing that the moral nature and the intellectual are really distinct functions, or rather groups of functions. These arguments, duly considered, will be found to be entitled to a certain weight in relation to the question now to be considered; for, if these two groups of functions are really distinct, it becomes probable that the organs of which they are functions are also distinct. Let us suppose this to be the case; let us also suppose that the higher cerebral ganglia are the physical basis of the intellectual nature; and now let us see if we can find any other organ of which the moral nature may be reasonably supposed to be the function.

There are some general considerations which are calculated to raise a presumption in an unbiased mind that there may be a closer connection than is usually supposed between the great sympathetic and the emotional nature.

1. In the first place, we feel that our emotions have their seat, not in our heads, but in our bodies; and the languages of all nations and of all times refer the emotions to the heart, in and about which organ are grouped the larger ganglionic masses of the great sympathetic system.

2. In the second place, the intellect is less developed and the moral nature more developed, in proportion to her whole mental volume, in woman than in man, and we know that the brain is smaller, and we have reason to think that the great sympathetic is larger, relatively to her size, in the female than in the male of our species. I do not think a comparison has ever been made by direct observation between the great sympathetic in man and the same organ in woman, but it has two large organs to supply in the female which do not exist in the male, viz.: the mammary glands and the uterus. It is certain, therefore, that the organ is larger in the female by that much at least.

3. In the third place, there is the fact that all the functions which we know of, as belonging without question to the great sympathetic, are what we may call by comparison with the functions of the cere-

bro-spinal nervous system continuous functions—for example: the control of the calibre of the arterial walls, the slow and almost constant peristaltic action of the bowels, the regulation of secretion and nutrition; while all the functions of the cerebro-spinal nervous system might be called, by contrast, instantaneous functions—the reception of sense impressions, the act of thought, the contraction of a voluntary muscle, or a group of voluntary muscles—these functions are scarcely begun before they are ended. Now, it is easy to see into which of these groups emotions naturally fall. We do not love for an instant, as we think of an algebraic equation or of a point in a business transaction, and then cease for a time, or altogether, to love; on the contrary, we love for hours, days, or weeks, continuously. So with hate. Though we do not hate, most of us, fortunately, quite as persistently as we love, still we seldom hate for a few seconds or even minutes only; we are apt to keep it up for hours, perhaps days. Faith, I consider to be, with love, the highest function of the moral nature. I do not mean anything like belief, when I say faith; belief belongs to the intellect—is a part of the intellectual nature. The moral function, faith (see p. 23 *et seq.*), is something that includes reliance, confidence, and courage, and when it is possessed in a large measure, and carried into matters of religion, the person possessing it is safe from at least half the ills of mortality. Without encroaching upon the domain of the theologian we may say in a true sense that such a man is saved. This faith, like love, is continuous for days, weeks, or months.

Look, now, at the more momentary passions, such as anger or fear. We know that to become angry takes an appreciable length of time, some seconds, minutes, or even hours, according to the degree of mobility of the individual nervous system acted upon, and according to the nature of the exciting cause of the anger, and that when the passion is fully aroused it continues for some time, sometimes for days, and then passes off slowly as it arises. The same may be said of fear. It is well known that after a great danger has been passed, fear will often last for days, and even weeks, and fear is never momentary.

4. A fourth consideration which argues a connection between the moral nature and the great sympathetic nervous system is what we may call the depth of both the one and the other. The great sympathetic is anatomically deep; it is buried out of sight; it does not come to the surface at any point; it has no direct connection, as far as we know, with the outside world. You know that in this respect it is in strong contrast with the cerebro-spinal nervous system, to which belong all the nerves of general and special sense, and which supplies all the muscles whose movements are visi-

ble on the surface, as well as the vocal organ. The great sympathetic has no such connections with the outside world at all; no sense organs, and no voluntary muscles belong to it; it has no vocal organ. Now, how does the great sympathetic compare in these respects with the moral nature? I say it tallies exactly with this latter. For whoever will consider a moment will see that we can neither receive nor transmit moral impressions directly as we can thoughts. We can only receive moral impressions by their spontaneous growth within us, as most often is the case with love or faith; or if we acquire them in a more casual manner, we get them through intellectual changes— for example: we see and realize a danger and we have fear; we perceive an insult and we become angry. The intellectual movement must precede the emotional movement. The emotional life is under the intellectual; as I said at first it is deeper. Now, as with receiving, so with transmitting or expressing emotional states. I can tell you that I am afraid or that I love. This, however, would not be an expression of an emotion. This would be only an issue of intellectual paper intended to represent emotional gold, which last never leaves the vault of the bank. It is true to a very large extent that we cannot express our emotions. We all feel and know this in every-day life. I said just now that the great sympathetic has no vocal organ. So, too, the moral nature was born dumb. If we do attempt to express an emotional state, we take roundabout or special ways to do it. For example: if I were very angry and wished to show it, or, perhaps, was compelled by my passion to show it without wishing it, I should do so by speaking in a loud voice, in a peculiar tone, by gesticulations, and by facial expressions; and even then, with all this fuss, I should not express my moral state as clearly and fully as I could express any given intellectual state by means of a few calm words.

5. A fifth general consideration is the simplicity of structure of moral states as compared with concepts. For a simple moral state, such as love or fear, unassociated with any idea, seems to be absolutely homogeneous, while (as said above, p. 18 *et seq.*) concepts, the simplest of them that we can reach by our best efforts of analysis, such as the idea of time, space, size, are undoubtedly extremely complex, being built up of elements which do not singly enter into consciousness, just as any piece of matter—a grain of sand for instance—is an exceedingly complex body, the ultimate atoms of which do not form objects of sense. Not only is this true, but the concepts in ordinary use are enormously complex, taking such concepts as those just mentioned as the unit of comparison. To make this clear, let us compare a simple moral state with an ordinary concept. A

mother loves her child. We have here a moral state—love—and a concept—the idea of the child; the union of these two makes the whole mental state which we are to consider. Now, I defy you to decompose love. It is, I am satisfied, absolutely homogeneous. But look at the concept—child. To form this mental image, an idea, shadowy, perhaps, but real, must be formed of each visible part of the child's body—legs, arms, neck, features, hair; and each of these concepts is made up of others—size, texture, shape, hardness or softness. Multiply one of these by the other and you have an immense number of concepts, which yet, perhaps, are not simple, but which would admit of still further analysis. And besides these there are numerous other concepts necessary to make up the concept, child—such as its dress, age, habits, manner, speech, history, and each of these are, in their turn, highly compound concepts; so that it would not be difficult to show that in that one concept—child—there enter hundreds of simpler concepts; and I believe that not one out of all those hundreds could be shown to be an absolutely simple concept. Now, the structure of the brain is infinitely more complex than the structure of the great sympathetic; so that the simplicity of moral states, compared with intellectual states, finds its parallel in the organs of which we suppose these two respectively to be functions. This parallel holds good in the other functions of these two nervous systems, but it is unnecessary to follow it out in detail in this place. But, consider for a moment, the immense number of sounds that the ear of a trained musician can receive and recognize at the same time, or the enormous number of objects that the eye can take cognizance of at once; consider the complexity of the functions of coördination of muscular movement, as in playing the piano; then turn to the functions controlled by the great sympathetic, such as secretion and nutrition, and see how homogeneous they are as compared with these functions of the cerebro-spinal system.

6. In the sixth place, let us consider what I shall call range of intensity. All moral states have a wide range in degree of intensity. Intellectual images, though they are more vivid at times than they are at others, have no true range of degree of intensity. Now, all the functions of the great sympathetic system have this capacity of varying in intensity well marked; and not only so, but the variation is very commonly associated with varying degrees of emotion. All the established functions of the great sympathetic have this property of variation. The lachrymal gland has a certain rate of secretion, which is sufficient to keep the eyeball moist. This rate is altered both by diminution and excess—that is, in intensity of activity of the function, under the influence of irritants and disease,

and especially under the influence of emotions, or rather, it would be more correct to say synchronously with the existence of emotion. The same thing is true of the gastric, urinary, intestinal, and, in fact, of all the other secretions—markedly of the mammary secretion and of the secretion of the testes. Variation in intensity of action of unstriped muscle, also synchronously with the existence of strong emotion, is not less marked, as seen in alterations of the heart's action, in excess and defect of peristaltic action of the muscular coats of the intestines, and in persistent contraction of the radiating fibres of the iris in terror and the continuous relaxation of them in rage. The same thing is true of nutrition, which has a wide range of variation of intensity, and also a general correspondence with the prevailing tone or state of the moral nature; for during times when nutrition is exceptionally active, as during the growth of the organism, or upon recovery from a disease which has reduced the weight of the organism, there is exceptional activity of the moral nature; and not only so, but at these times the positive functions—love and faith—are then especially active; and conversely, during the progress of wasting diseases and during the time that the organism is decreasing in weight in old age, when this decrease happens, the moral nature is exceptionally inactive and the negative functions prevail over the positive. On the other hand, this range of intensity does not belong to the intellect in the same sense at all. Mental images, as mentioned above, are certainly more vivid some times than they are at others; but this is a vastly different thing from the immense range of intensity of any one of the passions—as love, for instance—which may be merely a slight liking for some thing, animal, or person, or may be so intense in degree as to absorb into itself every form of energy belonging to the organism. And as this quality of range of intensity does not belong to the intellect, so neither does it belong to any other function of the cerebro-spinal system. The sense organs are passive instruments which merely receive what is offered them. We have, to be sure, a perception of different degrees of light and color, different degrees of taste and odor, different degrees of loudness of sound, and different degrees of pain, but these are the reports of passive organs of different degrees of stimulation from without the organism, and are not parallel with the different degrees of emotional excitement. The muscular system, too, stimulated by the motor tract of the cerebro-spinal nervous system, acts with greater vigor at one time and less at another, the muscular contractions being stronger or weaker. But this range of intensity, such as it is, depends itself chiefly if not entirely upon variations in the state of the moral nature;

for you know that it is impossible to make an extraordinary muscular effort unless there is some unusual emotional condition behind the effort and prompting it. And the elaborate intercommunication between the great sympathetic and the motor tract of the cord makes it quite clear to us how this connection between the emotional and motor functions is to be explained.

7. The seventh of these considerations which I have to urge is the relation which subsists between the size of the organism and the development of the moral nature. I believe that, as a rule, it is true that "small men have small minds." Not but that small men have as good intellectual qualities as full-sized men, but that they are inferior morally. There are many instances in the history of the race of men of great, even very great, intellectual power, who were at the same time under the medium size. Napoleon, Wellington, and Brougham are examples. There are also plenty of examples of low intellectual power in large men. But, as far as I know, there has been no example of a man of great moral elevation—a religious founder, a supreme artist—who has not been up to the ordinary standard of humanity both in height and weight. On the other hand, moral idiots, of whom I have known several, that is, men almost destitute of the higher, and deficient even in the lower, moral functions are always, as far as my experience of

them has gone, small, and often very small men, and the same thing has been remarked by others. It is worth noticing, in this connection, and in reference to the next clause of the argument that tall men live longer than short men. Now, as the great sympathetic undoubtedly governs nutrition, and as the brain has nothing to do with this function except in a very remote and indirect way, we can understand why a good development of the organism should accompany a high moral nature if we suppose that this is also a function of the great sympathetic, and why this relation should be wanting or at least little marked in the case of the intellectual nature. But, if we suppose that the moral nature is, as well as the intellectual nature, a function of the same part of the cerebro-spinal nervous system, then I do not see how we are to explain the general fact set forth in this paragraph.

8. The eighth general consideration is, I think, still more curious and cogent. It has to do with the relation which subsists between moral elevation and length of life. It seems that, other things being equal, those who have the best and highest moral natures live the longest. But, as length of life depends upon the degree of perfection of the great sympathetic nervous system, it follows that either the moral nature is a function of this organ or is related to it in some other intimate manner.

The argument is, first, other things being equal, those who have the best and highest moral natures live the longest; second, length of life depends upon the degree of perfection of the great sympathetic nervous system; thirdly, therefore, the moral nature is a function of the great sympathetic.

The first clause of the argument is, those who have the best and highest moral natures live the longest. I shall support this statement by four facts. The first of these four is the extraordinary longevity of the Jewish race, a race which, to use Richardson's language, "has not only endured the oppression of centuries without being lost, but as it now exists, scattered here and there over the earth in different countries, and among the most varied social and natural conditions, is of all civilized races the first in vitality."

This point will be found fully discussed in Richardson's last great work, *Diseases of Modern Life*. M. Neufville found that in Frankfurt the average duration of the life of the Jews was forty-eight years and nine months, and of the Christians thirty-six years and eleven months. The Civil State Extracts of Prussia give to the Jews a mortality of 1·61 per cent.; to the whole kingdom a mortality of 2·62 per cent. Taking into consideration all the data given by Richardson on this point, I estimate that the average life of the Jew is at least six or eight years longer than the average life of the non-Jewish inhabitants of the various countries in which the Jews live. Richardson says, on on another page of the same work—

> "Different causes have been assigned for this higher vitality of the Jewish race, and it were indeed wise to seek for the causes, since that race which presents the strongest vitality, the greatest increase of life, and the longest resistance to death, must, in course of time, become, under the influences of civilization, dominant. We see this truth, indeed, actually exemplified in the Jews; for no other known race has ever endured so much or resisted so much. Persecuted, oppressed by every imaginable form of tyranny, they have held together and lived, carrying on intact their customs, their beliefs, their faith for centuries, until, set free at last, they flourish as if endowed with new force. They rule more potently than ever, far more potently than when Solomon in all his glory reigned in Jerusalem. They rule, and neither fight nor waste. Happily, we have not far to go to find many causes for the high vitality of a race, which, by comparison with the Saxon and Celtic, is physically feeble. The causes are simply summed up in the term, 'soberness of life.' The Jew drinks less than his 'even Christian;' he takes, as a rule, better food; he marries earlier; he rears the children he has brought into the world with greater personal care; he tends the aged more thoughtfully; he takes better care of his poor, and he takes better care of himself. He does not boast of to-morrow, but he provides for it; and he holds tenaciously to all he gets. To our Saxon and Celtic eyes he carries these virtues too far; but thereby he wins, becomes powerful, and scorning boisterous mirth and passion, is comparatively happy."

The Jews, then, have an extraordinary amount of vitality. Why is this? The explanation of it which Richardson sees is that they lead a more moral life than other people. Now, in the first place, no one, it seems to me, can suppose that there is enough difference between the Jew's outward life and the Christian's to make this immense difference in longevity. And, in the second place, suppose there was, why should Jews lead better lives than Christians? That they do lead better lives I am prepared to believe. But why do they?

What makes each one of us live as good lives as we do live? I do not say that our lives are good, but we all know that they might be worse than they are. What makes them, then, as good as they are? Surely the elevation, such as it is, of our moral natures. Well, then, supposing the Jews' lives are better than our lives, it is a fair inference that their moral natures are, on an average, better, that is, higher than our moral natures—that with them love and faith are more developed, and hate and fear more restricted in proportion than with us. But although these considerations are entitled to a certain amount of weight, I do not propose to rest my argument upon them. I have surer ground. This ground is that the Jews have initiated the most advanced religions of the world during the whole course of its history. Jesus said: "Ye shall know them by their fruits. Do men gather grapes of thorns or figs of thistles?" Could a race with a low moral nature originate a high religion? That is like asking, has a man with a low moral nature a high moral nature? or is a short man tall? No one, I fancy, will dispute, if he is capable of understanding what he is talking about, that the race which produced the lawgivers, psalmists, prophets, and finally Jesus himself, was and therefore doubtless is, the race which possessed and possesses the supreme moral nature of this planet. Here, then, we have one instance of length of life associated with a high moral nature. This fact, standing alone, though it might raise a strong presumption in our minds of the connection I am seeking to establish, could not prove it. Without stopping to discuss how it might be evaded, let us go on to the second of the four facts I spoke of, which will be well calculated to support it.

There are two classes of great men. One of them is great by elevation of the moral nature; the other class is great by intellectual power. The first class is divisible into two sections. In the first section stand the leaders of our race in the eternal war against the powers of darkness. These are the men who are exceptionally endowed with the supreme faculty—faith. They are the great religious founders and innovators. The other section of this class comprises the men who come next after them as benefactors of humanity. These are the men who possess in fullest degree the divine faculty—love. These are the great artists, whether poets, musicians, painters, or sculptors. The second class of great men is also divisible into two sections. The first section is composed of the philosophers—men who are great by their power of abstract reasoning. The other section is made up of scientists—men who are great by development of what may be called the external faculties of the intellect, such as perception, conception, memory, and comparison.

Now, we all know that, although a man may

possibly have one or more of these classes of mental qualities highly developed, and the rest below the average, that this is not the rule. Usually, if faith is extraordinarily developed, love is at least well developed. And if the moral nature, as a whole, is of a first-class order, that the intellectual nature will be good and probably very good. And, conversely, that a first-class intellect implies, as a rule, a high if not a very high moral nature. There are two principal reasons why this must be true. The first is, that of whatever parts of the nervous system these two are functions, the organs to which they are thus related are closely allied, and a high development of the one will be almost certainly accompanied by a high development of the other. The second reason is, that the activity and efficiency of the intellectual nature is largely dependent upon the degree of development of the moral nature, which last is undoubtedly the driving power of our mental mechanism, as the great sympathetic is the driving power of our bodily organization. What I mean is, and I think that every one will agree with me here, that, with the same intellectual power, the outcome of that power will be vastly greater with a high moral nature behind it than it will be with a low moral nature behind it. In other words, that with a given brain a man who has strong and high desires will arrive at more and truer results of reflection than if, with the same brain, his desires are comparatively mean and low. We are safe, then, I think, in saying that, as a rule and on the average, a high moral nature implies a high intellectual nature ; and, conversely, that a high intellectual nature implies a high moral nature. When I had arrived at this stage of the argument in my own mind, I took a cyclopædia of biography, which, of course, contained the names of all the men and women who have lived in historical times noted for intellectual or moral greatness, and with the aid of my friend, Dr. Burgess, I took every age given in the book, with the exception of such as were manifestly errors by misprint or otherwise. I left out those, and such persons as Parr and Jenkins whose only title to admission to the cyclopædia was their extraordinarily long life. I left out, also, all ages over one hundred and twenty as probably exaggerated, though by doing this I no doubt lost several great ages. The result was remarkable. I got 13,534 ages from fifteen to one hundred and twenty years. Of these 13,534 people,

20	died between the ages of	15	and	20
91	"	"	20	"	25
205	"	"	25	"	30
341	"	"	30	"	35
435	"	"	35	"	40
568	"	"	40	"	45
776	"	"	45	"	50
1068	"	"	50	"	55

4*

1293	died between the ages of	55	and	60
1645	"	"	60	"	65
1693	"	"	65	"	70
1835	"	"	70	"	75
1445	"	"	75	"	80
1215	"	"	80	"	85
555	"	"	85	"	90
240	"	"	90	"	95
69	"	"	95	"	100
19	"	"	100	"	105
15	"	"	105	"	110
3	"	"	110	"	115
3	"	"	115	"	120

The average age of the whole number is 63·464 years, say 63½ years. Now, in estimating the value of this result, several considerations must be kept in view. On the one hand, we must recollect that a good many of these men, such as the great scientists and philosophers, had to live to forty or perhaps fifty years of age to get time to do the work which gave them admission to the cyclopædia, though a large number of men of this class died at ages from thirty years downward. On the other hand, we have to remember that many of these men were soldiers, sailors, missionaries, partakers in revolutions, martyrs, explorers, and, in a word, were in positions which frequently entailed an early death by violence. We must also remember that these men lived, many of them, in tropical and unhealthy countries, and many belonged to times and countries in which the average duration of life was not as great as it is in modern civilized nations. It is upon observation of these that our life tables are based. In spite of all these drawbacks, I find that in England the average age at death of magistrates, clergymen, merchants, gardeners, masons and bricklayers, surgeons, butchers, lawyers, joiners and carpenters, house-painters, millers and bakers, all of whom had to be taken at from twenty to fifty years old to start with, was only 54·72, say fifty-four and three-quarter years, against sixty-three and one-half years—the average age at death of our lives from the cyclopædia—a difference of eight and three-quarter years in favor of the latter. More than this, I took all the ages from the cyclopædia from fifty years upward, an age which would exclude almost totally our first consideration, which was, it will be remembered, that these men had to live to a certain age to do the work which entitled them to a place in the cyclopædia, but which would not, of course, exclude the opposite consideration, viz.: that these men lived in many times and countries, and often met violent deaths. I then compared the ages from fifty upward with what is called the English Life Table. I had eleven thousand and ninety-eight ages of fifty years and upward from the cyclopædia. I found that of that number three hundred and forty-nine passed the age of ninety—that is, one in every thirty-two. Now, according to the English Life Table, of four thousand six hundred and sixty-two men at fifty, only one hundred and fourteen pass the age of ninety—that is, one in every forty-one—an immense difference, as you see, especially when we consider the disadvantages above mentioned under which the men from the cyclopædia labor. I made comparisons many other ways, and all with the same result. There is no doubt that the average length of life of what we call great men is greater than it is among ordinary men, probably by six or eight years at the least.

Without stopping to comment further on this fact now, let us pass on to the third fact which we have to consider in this connection. This fact is that married men and women live longer—by some five years on an average—than men and women who are not married. The only reason assigned for this difference is that men pick the healthiest women to marry, and that women pick the healthiest men. Now, although I am willing to allow that this consideration is entitled to some weight, still I am satisfied it is more than balanced in the female sex by the loss of life incident to parturition; and strange to say, there is a greater difference between the length of life of married and single women than there is between the length of life of married and single men.

The real explanation of this fact from our present point of view lies on the surface. Why do men and women marry? In ninety-nine cases out of a hundred they marry because they love one another. This ought to be the sole reason for marriage, and it really is nearly the sole reason. If the capacity for loving in a given individual reaches a certain point, it is just about certain that that individual will marry, for two reasons. The first is, that given a certain capacity for loving, and the individual man or woman will seek to marry. And the rule holds here as in other matters, "Seek, and ye shall find." The second reason is, that nothing attracts love like love. No beauty, accomplishments, or wealth, make a man or woman half so attractive to the opposite sex as a loving heart. The result is, since the greater the capacity for love the better is the moral nature, that, on the average, the higher moral natures marry and the lower ones do not. So here again we find the higher moral nature associated with greater length of life.

The fourth and last fact is that women live longer than men by some two to four years on an average. The exact difference of length of life of women and men is not perhaps known; but it is certain that women live longer than men by about the time above mentioned. It is stated above (p. 65) that the moral nature is more and the intellectual less developed in women than in men, also that the great sympathetic is probably larger while the brain is certainly smaller in the female than in the male sex of our species. Now, is it true that the moral nature is higher in women than it is in men? I believe it is. And there is no doubt that the balance of opinion is in favor of this view. I believe women have, on an average, a greater capacity of love and faith than men have, and, on an average, a less capacity for hate and fear. The woman's excess of faith is shown chiefly in her superior power of endurance and her greater patience under suffering and ill-usage. In matters of religion I do not know that women have more faith than men; they certainly have a greater capacity of belief; but this, as we have seen above, is quite a different thing, and is due largely to the inferiority of their intellectual nature. I think there is no doubt that women surpass men in their power of loving. Maternal love has always, and I think justly, been considered the most intense and enduring of all forms of this passion. I believe all physicians will agree that women have less fear of death than men have. If this were granted it would almost follow that women have less fear than men. Finally, though one cannot prove such points as this, I am satisfied that women hate less than men do. Women are very subject to passing anger and petty spite, but they very seldom hate deeply. There are very few murders committed by women in comparison to the number committed by men, though women on an average have greater provocation to the commission of this act than men have, and fully as great facilities for its accomplishment. It is said that there is only one suicide committed by women for three committed by men; and that female criminals are in proportion to male criminals as one to five. But some one may say: If women have a higher moral nature than men have, how is it that there are no religious founders and so few supreme artists among the members of this sex? The reason is, that although the essential factor in a religious founder is faith, and in a supreme artist love, yet a high grade of intellect must go along with the high moral nature if anything great in either of these lines is to be achieved. Well, we know that the average weight of a woman's brain is forty-four ounces, against forty-nine and one-half ounces for the average weight of a man's brain; but the knowledge of this fact is not necessary to assure us that woman's intellect is very much below the level of man's. Lacking, therefore, one essential factor of greatness, woman cannot be great in the same way that the greatest men are great; but she can be great in the sense of being good, and in this sense she is greater than man. And so far as civilization has yet gone, which does not seem to me to be very far, women have been, and are, in the best and truest sense of the word, the acknowledged civilizers of the race.

Now, these four facts taken together are tolerably exhaustive. All men and women are either married or not married. All men are either Jews or not Jews. All men are either great or not great. And finally, the race is divided into men and women. If it is said that the longevity of the Jews is not connected with their high moral nature, but is an unexplained peculiarity of their race, I say, that explanation does not apply to the other three cases. And I say that I want an explanation that will cover all the facts. If it is said, as to the second case, that great moral and intellectual activity imply a high vitality, and therefore, on the average, a long life, I say that objection in part admits my argument, and that in part it is not true, for men on the whole are higher mentally than women, and yet women live longer than men. The fact is, the only thing that can be shown, as far as I can see, to be common to Jews, great men, married people, and women, as against non-Jews, ordinary men, unmarried people, and men, is a higher moral nature. In the three first cases there is, doubtless, along with the higher moral nature, a better intellectual nature, which, as I have shown, is a necessary accompaniment of the former in cases where the conditions are the same; but there is no visible connection between a good intellect and length of life. And in the last case this condition is reversed, for in women the intellectual nature is lower than in men, while the moral nature is higher and the length of life greater. If, however, you adopt the hypothesis that the moral nature is a function of the great sympathetic, there is a very plain connection between elevation of the moral nature and longevity; and what I say is, that to account for the facts you must adopt that hypothesis; for I say that the only explanation which will cover all the facts is that the moral nature, being a function of the great sympathetic, and the great sympathetic being *par excellence* the organ of vitality, longevity and moral elevation are necessarily connected.

The second clause of this argument need not detain us long. It is: Length of life depends on the degree of perfection of the great sympathetic. No one, I think, who realizes what the well-understood functions of the great sympathetic are, will deny that this proposition is almost self-evident, since it is known that this nervous system underlies and controls all the essentially vital functions, such as digestion, secretion, circulation, and, above all, nutrition. Death is really, in nine cases out of ten, due to —I might almost say is—failure of nutrition, therefore failure of the great sympathetic. For the degenerative changes which usher in and lead to death in old age, though they are more clearly seen by us to result from this cause, are really not more especially due to failure of nutrition than are many other conditions which lead to death.

It is my belief, then, that the arguments urged in this eighth general consideration, though they might not be conclusive of themselves, are entitled to very great weight when taken along with the other arguments contained in this chapter, and that they will go a long way toward persuading the attentive and unprejudiced reader that the moral nature is one of the functions of the great sympathetic.

In further considering this part of our subject, we have to look at the problem from two sides, the converse of each other. First, we have to consider the different ways emotions are caused or excited, and see whether these causes are such as act upon the cerebro-spinal nervous system or upon the great sympathetic. Then, secondly, an emotion being excited, we have to consider the expression of this emotion, that is, its effect upon the economy, and see whether those organs supplied by the sympathetic are primarily affected and most affected by the nervous disturbance which is the physical accompaniment of the emotion, or whether those organs supplied by the cerebro-spinal nervous system are those which are first and most affected.

We have, then, to consider, in the first place, emotional excitants, and to try to determine from their seat and nature which nervous system it is that they act upon in giving rise to an emotional state. Now emotions are aroused in three ways: first, spontaneously—from some condition of the body or part of the body; secondly, they are excited by thoughts through associations formed in the past either of the individual or of the race; thirdly, they are excited by impressions received through the senses without the intervention of thought.

A complete list of the instances in which emotions arise spontaneously, or from some condition of the body or part of the body, would be much too long to be recited here. I will first mention one or two physiological and then proceed to a few pathological conditions.

Let us first notice the relation which exists between age and the activity of the moral nature in general. In childhood and youth you know that there is a constant and rapid succession of emotional states. A healthy, active child is either in a state of joy or grief nearly all the time while awake. Boys and girls are almost constantly either playing, quarreling, or sulking; that is, there is some active emotional condition present nearly all the time. Young men and women—that is, very young men and women—are almost equally liable to this constant domination of one emotional state after another. Youth is the age of impulse and passion—it is the age of bad poetry in the male and of hysteria in the female. This law is as well exemplified in the lower animals as it is in man—lambs, kittens, puppies, and probably the young of all animals, are much more emotional than adults of the same species. But from childhood to maturity is not the age during which the higher centres of the cerebro-spinal nervous system are especially active. These children who are so fond of play and so apt to sulk, and these poetical young men and hysterical young women are not particularly either thoughtful or studious. There is, in fact, no reason to suppose that there is during this period any extraordinary activity of any of the higher cerebral centres. I say advisedly, " higher cerebral centres," because we know that in youth the sensory motor tract of the cerebro-spinal nervous system is more active than it is in later life. But we also know that there is a most elaborate and intimate connection between this sensory motor tract and the great sympathetic; and we know too, that the actions of childhood and youth are prompted more by emotional impulse than are the actions of mature men and women; so that the great activity of the sensory motor tract of the cerebro-spinal nervous system during this period of life does not necessarily tell against my argument.

It is a fact, then, that in youth, the moral nature is markedly more active than it is later in life, and it is a fact that the intellectual nature is not markedly more—that it is even less—active in youth than at maturity; and furthermore, it is a fact that the great sympathetic nervous system is very much more active in childhood and youth than it is afterward, as shown by its universally acknowledged functions—for instance, by the greater activity of all the secretions, by the greater activity of digestion, assimilation, and nutrition.

If then we join, as it seems to me that we must join, the excess of function to the more active organs the inference is plain—it is, that the moral nature is a function of the great sympathetic.

The next most prominent physiological condition which gives rise to an emotional state is undoubtedly that which underlies the development of sexual passion. The essential part of this condition is certainly an active and healthy state of the testes or ovaries; for if all the other conditions be present, and these organs alone be either absent or materially injured by disease, or immature, or atrophied, or if they be functionally inert from any other cause, this particular emotional state cannot be produced; while the absence or disease of no other organ will operate as a positive bar to its existence. The presence in the mind of the image of a person of the opposite sex, although to the unthinking it seems to be the chief factor in the production of this emotional state, has in reality nothing at all to do with it in any fundamental sense, for this emotion may exist without any such image being present, and, being fully aroused, it may in many people be readily transferred from one mental image to another, whereas if it were dependent upon the image this could not happen. It is in this way that we may account for those cases, frequently seen, in which a man, upon a very short acquaintance, marries a second woman, upon the breaking off of an engagement with a first. Again, in the higher animals—in whom we must admit a mental structure in sexual matters, almost, if not quite identical with our own—though some of them will not transfer their affections from one object to another, or will do so only with great difficulty, and after a certain period of mourning, yet in others there seems little or no cohesion between the mental image and the emotional state, so that the sexual glands being active, and the emotional condition in question being present, the individual upon whom the sexual favors may be bestowed is a matter, apparently, of entire indifference. These considerations seem to me conclusive against the theory that this emotional condition is dependent upon the mental image, and the reasons above given seem also to establish the position that the state of the sexual secreting glands is the real determining cause of the emotion. This being the case, we have next to ask, with which nervous system these glands are most intimately connected? You know what the answer to this question is. The ovaries receive no nerves but from the sympathetic, and the testes, as pointed out above, receive nerves from the cerebro-spinal nervous system only because they are exposed and require to be endowed with sensibility for their protection. But if the sympathetic nerves be the connecting link between the organ whose condition excites the emotion and the nerve centre in which that emotion arises, that centre must be the great sympathetic system.

The pathological conditions which give rise to active emotional states are extremely numerous, and I wish particularly, in this connection, to draw attention to the fact that it it is invariably in lesions of organs well supplied by the sympathetic that these perversions of the emotional nature occur. As a rule, in diseases of organs which are comparatively scantily supplied by the sympathetic, such as the bones, muscles, or lungs, there is little or no derangement of the moral nature; on the other hand, in diseases of the stomach, heart, liver, kidneys, suprarenal glands, and of the testes, ovaries, and uterus, there is always some, and often great, disturbance of the emotions. In cancer of the stomach, ulceration of the stomach, and chronic gastritis, there is a good deal of emotional disturbance. All physicians who have been much engaged in general practice have seen cases of dyspepsia in which constant low spirits and occasional attacks of terror rendered the patient's condition pitiable in the extreme. I have observed these cases often, and have watched them closely, and I have never seen greater suffering of any kind than I have witnessed during these attacks. Now, how do we know that these pathological conditions of the stomach produce terror and low spirits by impressions conveyed through sympathetic nerves to sympathetic ganglia and not by impressions conveyed through the pneumogastrics to the brain? We infer it because all the accompanying morbid phenomena are certainly due to disturbance of the sympathetic. Thus, a man is suffering from what we call nervous dyspepsia. Some day, we will suppose in the middle of the afternoon, without any warning or visible cause, one of these attacks of terror comes on. The first thing the man feels is great but vague discomfort. Then he notices that his heart is beating much too violently. At the same time, shocks or flashes as of electrical discharges, so violent as to be almost painful, and accompanied by a feeling of extreme distress, pass one after another through his body and limbs. Then in a few minutes he falls into a condition of the most intense fear. He is not afraid of anything; he is simply afraid. His mind is perfectly clear. He looks for a cause of his wretched condition, but sees none. Presently his terror is such that he trembles violently and utters low moans; his body is damp with perspiration; his mouth is perfectly dry; and at this stage there are no tears in his eyes, though his suffering is intense. When the climax of the attack is reached and passed there is a copious flow of tears, or else a mental condition in which the person weeps upon the least provocation. At this stage a large quantity of pale urine is passed. Then the heart's action becomes again normal, and the attack passes off. There is nothing imaginary about this description. It is taken word for word from the account given to the present writer by the actual sufferer, who is himself a highly intellectual medical man. Neither is the description a summary of a number of attacks, but it refers to one particular attack which was witnessed by the writer, and I am satisfied is absolutely accurate.

Now, what I wish to call attention to is, that all disturbance of function accompanying one of these attacks is disturbance of function presided over by the sympathetic. We have seen above that the secretions are controlled by this nervous system, and I have mentioned how the salivary, lachrymal, urinary, and cutaneous secretions are altered both by diminution and increase in these attacks. The heart's action is almost certainly under the control of the sympathetic, and it is greatly disturbed. The trembling, as more fully explained farther on, is probably the phenomenon produced when voluntary muscles are acted upon and thrown into action by the sympathetic nervous system. On the other hand we have no indication that, during the attack described, the cerebro-spinal nervous system is in any way excited or disturbed. The intellect is clear; the reasoning and perceptive faculties alike in perfect order; the control of the will over the voluntary muscles, through the medium of this nervous system, is in no way interfered with; and, in fact, so little is the centre of ideation involved, that, as I have stated, no mental image is associated with the emotion of terror—the man suffers simply from fear, not from fear of something. It seems, then, clear to me that the great sympathetic is the nervous system acted upon by the abnormal condition of the stomach, which nervous system in its turn reacts upon the economy, and consequently that the terror in question is one of its functions.

When the terror thus excited continues for some little time, it associates itself with an idea, and then the person affected is afraid of some definite thing happening (see p. 16); and it is very curious to notice how the fear attaches itself, not to the thing which the person has most cause to be afraid of, but to the ideas which occupy the most prominent place in his mind. Thus, among many cases of this kind known to me, where the condition in question is more or less chronic, I will cite three to illustrate this point. Case No. 1 is that of a priest, a good and wise man, and with him the terror is associated with the idea of endless misery, though he is well aware of the absurdity of this idea, or, at least, of the absurdity of his being especially exposed to this danger. Case No. 2 is a lawyer, and a very shrewd and successful business man; with him the terror is always associated with ideas of business mistakes and loss of money, though he scarcely ever made a business mistake in his life, and never lost any money, though he has made a great deal. Case No. 3 is a medical man of good ability, and with him the terror is always associated with ideas of sudden death, incurable disease, and poison, though he is a healthy man, and as little liable to be poisoned as any one living.

The lungs receive a very small supply of sympathetic nerves, and we know that long-continued disease of their tissue, ending in destruction of large parts of this tissue, and at last in death, will often scarcely give rise to low spirits, never to extreme depression or to violent emotion of any kind. The heart receives a very large supply of sympathetic nerves, and its diseases, as fatty degeneration of its substance, and calcareous degeneration of its arteries, are accompanied by very great depression of spirits, and often by agonies of anxiety and terror. Imperfections of the cardiac valves and contractions of the cardiac orifices are not, in the sense in which I am speaking, diseases at all; for there is in these cases no tissue change—there is simply a change in the mechanical conditions.

The liver is moderately well supplied with sympathetic nerves, and there is a moderate amount of disturbance of the moral nature in cases of disease of its tissue, as in cancer, and impairment of its functions, as in congestion; but as disease of the liver, either structural or functional, seldom or never occurs without structural disease or at least functional derangement of the stomach accompanying it, it is difficult to estimate the amount of the disturbance of the emotions caused by the hepatic conditions themselves.

Emotional conditions excited by disease of the kidneys are undoubtedly due, in great part, to the destructive changes going on in these organs, but they are also, to a certain extent, due to the uræmic poisoning which necessarily accompanies them, and so the effects of the blood change and of the organic change mask one another.

But the pathological condition most clearly in favor of my present argument is, beyond question, Addison's disease of the suprarenal glands. The number and size of sympathetic nerves sent to these small bodies is extraordinarily great. Moreover, they receive no cerebro-spinal nerves at all. Any one who has ever seen cases of this disease is aware of the extraordinary effect produced by disease of these bodies upon the moral nature. Long before the patient is obliged by the degree of his illness to abandon his usual occupations, he is greatly troubled with listlessness, languor, and low spirits, and as the disease advances these symptoms increase, and attacks of terror and extreme low spirits are common.

Now, to return to our old argument. The morbid action is in the suprarenal gland. The nerves which convey the impressions which excite emotional disturbance are necessarily here sympathetic nerves. The nerve centre in which the emotional disturbance takes place is therefore one or more sympathetic ganglia. Therefore the sympathetic ganglia are the nervous centres of emotional states.

In the second place, emotions are excited by thoughts through their associations with them, such associations having been formed in the past history of the individual, or much more often in the past history of the race of which he is a member. As this clause has nothing to do with the physical basis of the moral nature it is not treated in this place. Reference to this subject, which is too large to be fully considered in this essay, will be found at p. 33 *et seq.;* it is also incidentally touched upon in many places throughout this volume.

The third and last class of emotional excitants which we have to consider consists of sense impressions acting upon the moral nature without the intervention of thought. The nerves of the special senses lead from the periphery directly to the cerebro-spinal nervous centres. So, as a rule, when sense impressions are followed by mental states, which last are aroused by them, the first phase of the mental state is a thought—the realization by consciousness that something is occurring or exists in the outer world ; and if an emotion is excited, it is so secondarily, by the association in the past of the idea directly excited with the emotion which is excited in the second place. This rule holds good, as regards the senses of sight and touch, more absolutely than as regards the other senses, and it is more true of sight than of any other sense.

The impressions received through the sense of taste can hardly be said, as a general thing, to excite thought. They do excite a sort of emotion. The sense of smell varies greatly in different individuals in its power of exciting thought or emotion. Oliver Wendell Holmes describes wonderfully well how in some people it calls up emotions. In others this sense excites ideas very readily, so that they can name a drug or other odorous body more readily from its smell than from its look. Others again cannot name the commonest things from their odor. The excitation of this sense with them awakens a pleasant or a disagreeable sensation, and the effect stops there.

But the sense of hearing stands apart from the other senses in the degree to which it is capable of transmitting impressions directly to either the centres of intellectual or emotional life. Our knowledge of the anatomy of the nervous system is not minute enough to enable us to say why there exist these differences between the senses; why, for instance, sight awakens only ideas, and hearing either ideas or emotions according to certain differences in the sounds. We know that if we trace the optic nerves inward we find that they arise, by means of the optic tracts, from the posterior and superior part of the mesocephale, and are more or less connected with other parts of the brain in that neighborhood. If we trace the portio mollis of the seventh inward we find that it divides into two roots, one of which passes deeply into the central part of the medulla oblongata, the other winds around the corpus restiforme to the floor of the fourth ventricle. In this connection it is worthy of remark that the auditory ganglion from which the portio mollis springs is the lowest down of all the ganglia of the medulla oblongata; it is, therefore, the most contiguous of all the intercranial ganglia to the larger masses of the great sympathetic; this fact increases the likelihood of some closer relation between the roots of the auditory nerve and the great sympathetic than obtains in the cases of the other nerves of special sense—but it proves nothing. But if it were possible to trace the roots of this nerve, and if upon tracing them to their origin it were found that one of them belonged to, or had intimate connection with, the great sympathetic, while the other belonged to the cerebro-spinal system, a most important link in the chain of my argument would be supplied. But we cannot say that this is the case. Failing in this anatomical proof of a special connection between the auditory nerve and the great sympathetic, is there anything else about this nerve that would make us think that it contained sympathetic fibres? There is one thing. The auditory nerve is exceptionally soft in texture for a cerebro-spinal nerve—hence its name, "portio mollis;" and we know that sympathetic nerve trunks are softer in texture than the trunks of cerebro-spinal nerves. This fact might lead us to suspect that in the "portio mollis" there are sympathetic fibres mixed with cerebro-spinal fibres, but it can do no more than awaken such a suspicion.

Now, as to the sense of hearing itself. All the infinite variety of sounds that strike upon the human ear may be divided, according to their effect upon the human organism, into two great classes—those, namely, which primarily excite thought, and those which primarily excite emotion. The noise of a carriage on the street, of fowl in the yard, of steamboats and trains passing—these and thousands of other ordinary sounds simply excite a mental recognition of what the sound proceeds from. But if you lie under pine trees on a summer's day, and hear, without listening, the wind sigh and moan through the boughs, the emotional nature is moved irrespectively of any idea that may be excited. So, at the bedside of a sick child, its moans and cries of pain affect us quite out of proportion to, and irrespective of, the value our minds may set upon them; for, even if we know that the child is not dangerously ill, nor suffering very much, still we cannot prevent, as is said in common language, its cries going to our heart. And they do go to the heart, or at least to the nervous centre of the emotional nature, direct. So a cry of pain or distress, heard suddenly, awakens a corresponding emotion in the hearer before any thought is aroused.

The types of these two classes of sounds are, on the one hand, spoken language, and, on the other hand, music. The former we know appeals directly to the intellect, and does or does not arouse emotion, according as the thought awakened is or is not associated with an emotional state. The latter we also know appeals directly to the emotions, and only awakens thought secondarily, if it does so at all. Now, does that class of sounds which appeals directly to the moral nature, possess any quality which the other class does not possess, which would make us think that it, rather than the latter, acts upon the sympathetic? It has three such qualities, namely, continuity, rhythm, and range of intensity. We have seen above (p. 65 *et seq.*) that continuity is one characteristic of moral states as distinguishing them from intellectual states; we have seen also that it is a characteristic of the functions of the great sympathetic nervous system as distinguishing them from the functions of the cerebro-spinal nervous system. A moment's reflection makes it clear that continuity is also a characteristic of sounds that awaken emotion as distinguished from sounds that awaken thought. It is seen in such sounds as the murmur of wind through trees, the roar of waves on the beach—but it is especially noticeable in music and poetry; in these the successive waves of sound are made to depend upon one another, so that the parts of each clause of the music or poem are interdependent, and require to be read, sung, or played through in order that the full effect intended may be produced. So, secondly, all music is rhythmic, and all language which appeals most directly to the emotions, that is to say, all poetry, is also rhythmic. Now, rhythm is one of the leading qualities of the functions of the great sympathetic. All motions governed by it are rhythmic—the heart's motion, the peristaltic motion of the intestinal canal, and the contractions of the uterus in labor. I myself have no doubt that the period of utero-gestation, the determining cause of which has puzzled the world so much, as well as the periodic recurrence of ovulation, are both due to the same cause, namely, the rhythm or periodicity of function of the great sympathetic nervous system. Doubtless the chief advantage of regularity of time in taking meals is due to the fact that the gastric and salivary glands, and other organs concerned in digestion, being governed by the sympathetic, their functions are best performed rhythmically. The rhythmic, daily rise and fall of temperature, both in health and disease, is another example of the rhythm of a function which is under the control of this nervous system. And, thirdly, musical tones possess a quality which corresponds closely with what I have called range of intensity (p. 71, *et seq.*), and this seems to me to form another link between them and the great sympathetic nervous system.

We have finally to consider the expression of the emotions, to see if we can determine from which nervous system these phenomena proceed. It will not be necessary for our purpose here to discuss the whole of this branch of the inquiry, and I shall limit the few remarks I have to make to the expression of joy, grief, hate, fear; to the expression of, or if the term be preferred, the effect of, long-continued, excessive passion of any kind; and to a summary of the whole subject of the expression of the moral nature.

If joy is at all marked in degree it alters the heart's action; if excessive and sudden it arrests it momentarily; if more moderate in degree it makes it more frequent and stronger. Excessive joy causes pallor for a short time, and then slight flushing; moderate joy heightens the complexion. If joy is at all extreme it excites lachrymation in persons of mobile nervous organization. Sudden and great joy destroys the appetite, apparently by checking the salivary and gastric secretions; moderate joy stimulates the appetite, doubtless by exciting the secretions which assist in digestion.

Now, all the above are disturbances of functions which are controlled by the sympathetic; but we know that joy also gives rise to movements of various kinds—for instance, laughter, clapping of the hands, stamping of the feet, which are performed by voluntary muscles under the control of the cerebro-spinal nervous system. The peculiarity of these movements is that they are all rhythmical, and we know what a tendency there is for the functions of the sympathetic to be performed rhythmically. And further, they are all objectless; the intellect takes no cognizance of them, and no purpose or intention underlies them.

Now, I do not mean to argue that it is the

great sympathetic which excites the muscles to action in the production of these movements; but what I would suggest is that the great sympathetic, being the nervous system primarily excited, it excites the cerebro-spinal system by means of its elaborate connection with the latter, and the cerebro-spinal system acting under the influence of the great sympathetic, the character of the action of the former is stamped by the influence of the latter.

Grief is expressed by tears, pallor, loss of appetite—phenomena which belong to functions under the control of the sympathetic; by sobbing, wringing of the hands, and swaying to and fro of the head and body—motions which are under the control of the cerebro-spinal nervous system, and which are rhythmical. Excessive grief kills. I have known of one death, which will be referred to again in Chapter V., and which was plainly due to this cause. The fatal result of grief is due to interference with nutrition or with the heart's action, the event in either case being brought about through the sympathetic.

Hate or rage, if intense, is marked by pallor and partial arrest of the heart's action; if moderate, by flushing; if considerable, but still not intense, the flushing is extreme, the face becomes purple, the veins of the neck and forehead swell. Monkeys, as well as men, are said to redden with passion. Some authors say the pupils always contract in rage, and this we can easily understand; for if the muscular coat of the arteries be relaxed, as it is shown to be by the distension of the vessels, which causes the flushing, then the radiating fibres of the iris, which are also supplied by the sympathetic, would be equally in a semi-paralyzed state, and the circular fibres, which are supplied by the third nerve, would have less than usual to antagonize their ordinary tonicity, and the pupils would contract. In great rage there is often trembling. This phenomenon I shall consider further under the head of fear. The above-mentioned are the primary signs of rage, and they are all functional changes effected through the sympathetic. Other signs of rage, such as snarling, setting the teeth, clenching the fists, are manifestly secondary. They result from an intention in ourselves, or in our ancestors, to do something in consequence of rage, and are not the direct effect of the passion itself.

The disturbances of function which accompany fear are frequent and feeble action of the heart, pallor, and dilatation of the pupils. And I wish particularly to remark that whereas in rage there is flushing of the face and contraction of the pupils, as I have shown above, in fear there is pallor of the face and dilatation of the pupils—the muscular coats of the arteries and the radiating fibres of the iris, being both supplied by the sympathetic, are both stimulated to contract under the influence of terror, and are both relaxed in rage. In fear there is also suppression of the salivary and gastric secretions, extreme dryness of the mouth, and complete abeyance of the appetite; there is frequently increase, sometimes very marked, of the urinary and intestinal secretions.

Trembling is one of the most characteristic signs of fear. This is a movement of the voluntary muscles; but it is not a voluntary movement, the will having no control whatever over it. Trembling occurs in other emotional conditions besides fear, as in joy and rage. The shaking of ague, though not associated with any emotional state, is, I have no doubt, closely connected with emotional trembling. No author with whose works I am acquainted gives any explanation of this phenomenon. Were I to attempt an explanation myself, it would be that trembling is the peculiar movement of the voluntary muscular tissue when thrown into action, not by its own proper nervous system, the cerebro-spinal, but by the sympathetic. And I would argue that this was the correct view of the case—first, because it is certain that trembling occurs when the sympathetic is highly excited; secondly, because the cerebro-spinal system cannot, as far as we know, cause such a movement, and cannot control it when caused; and thirdly, because of its peculiar rhythmical character, which allies it to other movements originating in the sympathetic.

With regard to the sweating of great fear I have no explanation to give. I will simply remark that when, by division of sympathetic trunks, a part of the surface is to a great extent deprived of its connection with the sympathetic centres, that part of the surface is bathed in sweat.

I have quoted very few experiments upon the sympathetic in this essay, for the reason that I put very little confidence in the deductions drawn from them. To divide large sympathetic trunks, or to remove large sympathetic ganglia, must cause a disturbance of the general system which would necessarily mask to a great extent the peculiar effects flowing from the lesion of the nerves operated on; and any one who has paid attention to the literature of this subject cannot have failed to notice how contradictory are the positions supposed to be established by these means. Without denying that experiments may in the future throw light on this branch of physiology, I think it is safe to say that they have thrown very little upon it yet.

If there is one fact in relation to the functions of the great sympathetic better established than any other, it is that this nervous system controls the process of nutrition. Now, let us consider for a moment what a curious relationship exists between the process of nutrition and the habitual state of the moral nature. The best observer of man that ever lived on this planet makes *Cæsar* say to *Antony* :

> " Let me have men about me that are fat.
> . . . .
> Yond' Cassius hath a lean and hungry look.
> He thinks too much. Such men are dangerous."

Shakespeare says, what we all know, that men in whom dwell a preponderance of evil passions, such as hate, envy, jealousy, are, as a rule, ill nourished. The converse of this is as notorious, so that fat and jolly go together as naturally as do any two terms in the language. Not only does this general law hold, though liable to many exceptions from the operation of other laws interfering with it, but we find it equally true that any long-continued, inordinate passion, be it sexual love, hate, envy, or grief, is capable of influencing nutrition in a marked manner. Long-continued thought does not produce any such effect. If it seems to do so sometimes, it is because the student deprives himself of air, exercise, and sleep, in his ardent devotion to knowledge. Newton was as fat when he finished the *Principia* as when he began it. The writing of the *Novum Organum* did not reduce Bacon's weight a pound. Shakespeare, in whose splendid brain fermented all the ideas of his time—and it was a time, perhaps, of more ideas than the present, much as we pride ourselves in this respect—was a well-nourished man. The moral natures of Newton and Bacon were calm and serene. Shakespeare's heart glowed with a genuine love of humanity. If the moral nature be, equally with the intellectual, a function of some part of the cerebro-spinal nervous system, why are the undoubted functions of the great sympathetic so intimately connected with the former and so entirely unconnected with the latter?

The expression of the emotions, as seen above, is divided naturally into two classes of phenomena. One class consists of disturbance of functions presided over by the sympathetic; the other of disturbance of functions presided over by the cerebro-spinal nervous system. Some years ago, while reading an able work on this subject, I was much struck by the singular ingenuity and success with which the author traces the latter class of phenomena to intentional actions in remote progenitors, which actions had at last become habitual, or, as we say, instinctive, and often, under changed circumstances, meaningless. While, on the other hand, in the case of the former class of phenomena, either no attempt was made to trace the action, or, if it were made, it failed. The author did not himself seem to perceive the line which he thus unconsciously drew, and the fact of his not seeing it makes his indication of it the more instructive. It seems to me that the expression of the emotions should be divided into two great classes of acts, or, rather, two classes of alteration of functions—*i. e.*, alteration of functions presided over by the sympathetic, and alteration of functions presided over by the cerebro-spinal nervous system. The first class of phenomena is the most fundamental. It consists chiefly in alterations of secretion, nutrition, and circulation. The alterations of secretion are alterations of excess, defect, and perversion. Alterations of excess are seen in the profuse lachrymation of grief, in profuse secretion of the intestinal glands and kidneys in fear. Alterations of defect are seen in arrest of the salivary and other digestive secretions in fear, grief, and rage. Alteration of perversion is seen specially in the case of the mammary secretion, which is often altered in rage and fear so as to disagree with the infant, and sometimes sufficiently to cause the death of the child. The alterations of nutrition are alterations of excess and defect. Alteration of excess is seen when a person gains weight under the influence of tranquil happiness, while all other circumstances of the person's life remain the same. Alteration of defect is seen when a person loses weight from the influence of any depressing or inordinate passion. The alterations of circulation are alterations of excess, defect, and perversion. Alterations of excess are seen in the excessive action of the heart in rage, fear, or sudden joy, in the flushing of joy or love, the reddening of rage, or the blushing of shame. Alterations of defect are seen in the pausing of the heart in sudden terror, the depression of the heart's action in continuous grief, and in the pallor of fear. Alteration of the circulation by perversion is seen in intermittent cardiac action from excessive fear or rage.

The second class of alteration of functions—that is, alteration of functions presided over by the cerebro-spinal nervous system—may be divided roughly into alteration of functions presided over by the cord, and alteration of functions presided over by the brain. In the first class are a large number of quite meaningless acts, such as laughter, sobbing and sighing, clapping the hands in joy, wringing them in grief, stamping the feet in rage, swaying the head and body in despair. The two chief things to notice about these acts are that they are rhythmical, and that they are without intention. Now, if the cord was prompted to excite the muscles to these acts by the brain, that being the seat of the emotion, the probability seems to be that the acts would have some intention underlying them, and I see no reason why they should be rhythmical. But if the great sympathetic is the seat of the emotion, and if it prompts the cord to excite the muscles to these actions, then we can see both why the acts should be meaningless and why they should be rhythmical. Lastly, alteration of functions presided over by the brain are acts, as I think, equally prompted by the great sympathetic, but by the great sympathetic acting through the higher centres of the cerebro-spinal nervous system—that is to say, through consciousness. In this class of actions the intellect intervenes between the emotion and the act. These acts, performed by many generations in succession, and under changing circumstances, are apt to become meaningless, though they must have all had a meaning at one time; they also, by constant repetition, become involuntary and automatic. Such an act is the sneer of scorn or anger, in which the canines are partially uncovered—an act which originated when the canines were used by our ancestors under the influence of such passions. The involuntary setting of the teeth and clenching of the hands in rage, when there is no intention to enter into a physical contest—when, perhaps, the object of the passion is miles away—is a similar act. But though the acts of the class now under consideration may become meaningless, as shown above, as a class they are not meaningless acts, for this class comprises most of the acts of every-day life, the majority of which are prompted more or less remotely by some passion or emotion. Now, these acts as a class are remote from the moral state which excites to their performance, while the actions of the cord, and still more of the sympathetic, are instant upon the occurrence of the passion or emotion, showing that alteration of functions presided over by the great sympathetic is, so to speak, closest to the emotion; that alteration of function presided over by the spinal cord is next closest to the emotion; and that alteration of function presided over by the brain is most remote from the emotion. All these considerations tend to prove that the seat of the emotions is the ganglia of the great sympathetic and not the convolutions of the brain.

For, consider—if the brain was the organ of the moral nature, as it is of the intellectual nature, would not conscious intentional acts and ideational changes be the most instant and fundamental effects consequent upon the occurrence of a given emotional state? Would not meaningless actions, having their immediate source in the spinal cord—such as laughing, sobbing, stamping—come after these in degree of directness? And would not actions or alteration of functions having their immediate source in the ganglia of the great sympathetic—such as contraction and relaxation of unstriped muscle and alterations of secretion—would not these be less instant and direct than the other two classes of actions instead of being markedly more so?

In conclusion, were I to attempt to draw a comparison in a few words between the functions of the cerebro-spinal nervous system and those of the great sympathetic, I should say that whereas the cerebro-spinal nervous system is an enormous and complex sensory motor apparatus, with an immense ganglion, the cerebrum, whose function is ideation, superimposed upon its sensory tract, and another, the cerebellum, whose function is the coördination of motion, superimposed upon its motor tract, so the great sympathetic is also a sensory motor system without any superimposed ganglia, and its sensory and motor functions do not differ from the corresponding functions of the cerebro-spinal system more than its cells and fibres differ from those of this latter system, its efferent or motor function being expended upon unstriped muscle, and its afferent or sensory function being that peculiar kind of sensation which we call emotion. And as there is no such thing as coördination of emotion, as there is coördination of motion and sensation, so in the realm of the moral nature there is no such thing as learning, though there is development. And the moral nature of the ignorant man or uneducated woman may be, and often is, superior to the average moral nature of the cultivated members of our race.

Upon this view of the relative functions of the two great nervous systems, the only efferent function of the great sympathetic is stimulation of unstriped muscle; and we should have to view its influence upon secretion and nutrition as due to its power of contracting, or allowing to dilate, the coats of arteries. And this is in all probability very near the truth. Looked at in this way, the bulk and complexity of structure of each nervous system seems to correspond with the scope of its supposed functions; for the sensory motor functions of the cerebro-spinal system, including ideation and coördination of motion, would be as much in excess of the functions of the great sympathetic nervous system in amount and complexity as are the ganglia of the former in excess of those of the latter in complexity of structure and bulk.

6

CHAPTER IV.

IS THE MORAL NATURE A FIXED QUANTITY?

"Mein Freund, die Zeiten der Vergangenheit
Sind uns ein Buch mit sieben Siegeln;
Was ihr den Geist der Zeiten heist,
Das ist im Grund der Herren eigner Geist,
In dem die Zeiten sich bespiegeln."—GOETHE.

It is the purpose of this chapter to determine whether the moral nature is or is not a fixed quantity; that is to say, have the successive generations of men the same capacity of emotion? And not only so, but have they the same capacity of each of the functions of the moral nature? As before, we will keep to the four central functions—Love, Faith, Hate, Fear. Does the average modern man of a civilized nation love, trust, hate, and fear as much as and not more than the average man of the nearest approach to a civilized nation of (say) five thousand years ago? Is the moral nature now undergoing modification? Will the average man of five thousand years hence love, trust, hate, and fear equally with the average man of to-day? I cannot find that this question has ever, so far, been squarely faced and honestly studied. It seems to have been taken for granted that man's moral nature is a fixed quantity. What is the reason of this? There are several reasons for it. In the first place, let us put the question somewhat differently, so as to look at it from the ordinary point of view. Let us ask, Is the world becoming more moral? The former question underlies this latter question, and the difficulties in the way of answering the latter question will also be difficulties in the way of answering the former question. What are these difficulties? The first difficulty is that men are by no means agreed as to what constitutes moral advance. Many would say that it consists in a greater number and amount of good actions performed. The great difficulty about this answer is that people are very far from unanimous as to what constitutes good actions. To take some extreme cases of divergence of opinion on this point, it may be mentioned that a Thug considered assassination a good action; an Indian widow thought burning herself equally good; a Figian has no doubt of the propriety of killing his father or mother when they begin to grow old; the American Indian has always looked upon horse-stealing and scalp-taking as most laudable acts; our ancestors who lived near the border line between England and Scotland held very similar views; the early Inquisitors are said to have been among the best of men, and there can be no doubt that they thought they were doing good service to humanity in founding and maintaining the Inquisition, yet a great many, both at the time and since, have differed from them very widely upon this point.

Another definition of moral advance would probably be that it consists in an increase of certain qualities, half moral and half intellectual, such as charity, loyalty, hospitality, generosity. This definition would be open to the same objection as the last, inasmuch as these qualities are of such a practical and concrete nature that they can scarcely be considered apart from the actions which directly belong to them; and as soon as we get into the domain of action there will be a great diversity of opinion as to whether the action is good or not. It has often been argued, for instance, that charity considered as an action does more harm than good, and a strong case may be made out on this side. It is said that it tends to destroy the feeling of independence in the recipient, and that it is very injurious to him to have this feeling impaired; it is further said to discourage industry and to encourage servility in the dependent class. It is said again that the practice of this habit injures those who practice it—that it increases their self-esteem—that it makes them self-righteous—that it produces and deepens in their minds the feeling that they belong to a superior class of humanity to that to which those relieved by them belong—and it is said that this feeling is antagonistic to the feeling of universal brotherhood which is one of our highest ideals in the field of morality.

Parallel arguments have been used against loyalty. It is said that this feeling has often enabled kings to carry on unjust wars, which wars have done incalculable evil—that it has often blinded the eyes of the people of one nation to superiority in the people of other nations in matters of religion, philosophy, arts, mechanical inventions, and many other things, which better views and processes they might have adopted to their great advantage had they not been so blinded. Loyalty, indeed, though conceived by many to be one of the superior virtues, is considered by others, as well qualified to judge, as a form of selfishness and not a virtue at all. Similar considerations apply to the other so-called virtues of this class. 'What,' then, would constitute moral advance? This will appear presently. All I wish to show here is that men are not agreed upon this point, and that being the case they could hardly agree upon there being such a thing as moral advance at all.

In the second place, when the moral condition of a people is low, their ideal of moral perfection is also low, and as fast as their actual moral state improves, or even faster, their moral ideal advances. So that it is a fact that the lower or more degraded an individual, a tribe, or a nation may be, the less do they think about their moral condition, and the more are they satisfied with it when they do concern themselves about it. And whereas, among people of refined habits and virtuous lives, it is not uncommon to find men and women ready to acknowledge themselves the vilest sinners, this feeling I believe does not exist, even as an exceptional phenomenon, among barbarous tribes, such as the Figians, Australians, or lower tribes of Africans. The ideal of moral perfection among them being very little higher than their actual moral condition, as shown by the character of the gods they imagine to exist, there is no such wide difference, as with us, between how they really live and how they feel they ought to live; what we call conscience, therefore, troubles them much less than it does us. And as this law holds good with individuals as well as with races and nations, so it may be laid down as a rule which admits of very few exceptions that the really good man suffers much more from the upbraidings of his conscience than does the most depraved criminal. The tendency of this law is plainly to conceal from the higher races any advance in morality which they may have made, and to prevent the advance from being recognized.

A third reason why an advance in morality, supposing it to exist, would be difficult to recognize is that we have very imperfect means of judging of the degree of moral elevation attained by our ancestors at any given past time. We know tolerably well, in the case of several ancient nations, what they thought and what they did ; we know also what they taught in the way of morality, but as for their moral state we know very little about it. What I mean by their moral state being their habitual state of feeling toward one another—toward their wives and husbands—their children and parents—toward their slaves and the lower animals—toward external nature and their gods—toward death—and generally toward the infinite unknown which surrounded them as it surrounds us. About this, the habitual state of their feelings toward their entire surroundings, which in the aggregate makes up a man's moral state or condition, we can learn very little whether we study the ancient Jews, Greeks, Romans, Hindoos, or Egyptians. In the case of all these ancient people, the general impression is that their moral condition was lower than our own, and I have no doubt that this is true. Still, many men who ought to be well qualified to judge, as far as the study of extant records will qualify any one, will doubt the correctness of this view. If, instead of going back so far, we make the comparison between the present time and times of which the records are more complete than in the case of those referred to, then the interval is not sufficiently long to allow of any considerable change having taken place. We could not expect for instance that there would be a marked advance in man's moral state since the time of Elizabeth; manners and fashions have changed since then—men feel very differently now in many respects from the way men felt then—many of the associations between moral states and ideas have altered since that day, some absolutely, some only in degree —but, on the whole, very few would say that men felt less then than they do now, or on the whole felt less nobly. Many would say that the men of that age felt more than we, and more nobly.

It seems to me that the question: "Is the moral nature a fixed quantity?" has not been answered because it has not been properly asked. The usual form of the question is: "Is mankind becoming better?" or "Are men more or less moral now than they were formerly?" Asked in this way the question is always understood to involve, if not to deal principally with, acts as well as feelings; and even, singularly enough, in dealing with the question in this form, ideas of morality have been mistaken for morality itself. In thus dealing with the moral nature combined with the active and intellectual natures, the problem becomes insoluble from its extreme complexity. But it has been shown above (p. 14 *et seq.*) that neither the active nature nor the intellectual nature has anything to do with morality in any fundamental sense—that, in other words, they are apart from and outside of the moral nature. Let us then ask this question so as to confine both question and answer within the scope of the moral nature itself, and let us see if in that way we shall not be more successful in answering it. As before, we will consider, for the sake of simplicity, that love, faith, hate, and fear constitute the whole of the moral nature, and even if they do not they constitute so large a part of it that the question and answer can be based on them just as well as if there were no other moral states. The question then is: Are the quantities of each and all of these elements fixed? Do men on the whole to-day love, trust, hate, and fear as much as and no more than they did in the past? And will they in the future—the conditions of existence being the same—always go on loving, trusting, hating, and fearing as much as and no more than at present? This question, I believe, admits of a reliable answer.

The first thing which we have to take into account is the relation of the four functions of the moral nature to one another. It is plain at the outset that they constitute two pairs, and that the two elements of each pair are directly antagonistic to one another; these two pairs are love and hate, and faith and fear. Now, given a moral nature of a certain scope, and you cannot increase love in it without lessening hate, both relatively and absolutely. So hate cannot be increased without lessening love, or increase of faith cannot take place without lessening fear, or increase of fear without lessening faith. Then, again, love and faith are related to one another by affinity, so that one of them cannot, except as an exceptional phenomenon, be increased without increasing at the same time the other. The same may be said of hate and fear.

There are three modes by which we may attempt to trace the moral nature through the ages during which man has inhabited the earth with the view of forming an opinion as to whether it alters in the course of successive generations, and if so in what manner it alters. The first is the direct method, and is, perhaps, the most unsatisfactory of the three: it consists of going back in time, by the aid of documents and works of art, and by the aid of all means which are accessible to us, and tracing the actual development itself. The second consists in examining the various races of man: it rests on the supposition that in the course of development the higher races of to-day have passed through the same or very similar phases to those represented at the present time by the various inferior tribes and races of men; it is probable that a rough approximation to the real progress made may be observed in this way. The third mode consists in observing the mental development of the child from birth to maturity: this method draws its authority from the theory that, as the development of man in his intrauterine life is an abridged and somewhat imperfect representation of the development of animal life from the lowest forms of life up to man, so the mental development of the individual man is a rough representation of that of the race. By a careful examination, as far as it can be carried out, of these three lines of indications, by comparing the results reached in each, and by checking the one by the other, a history which would approximate more or less closely to the truth could no doubt be written; a history which, in its great outlines, could not but be essentially true. It is far from being my intention to write such a history as is here indicated. Such an attempt, to be made without extravagant presumption, would suppose on the part of whoever made it infinitely greater learning than I am possessed of. Neither is it necessary for my present purpose to write such a history here—a few hints, a few suggestions, are all that I can give, and I believe they will be sufficient both to make plain my line of argument and also to support it sufficiently.

In the first place, then, let us see what we can learn from an examination of the moral nature of our ancestors. Those of us who adopt the development hypothesis would begin and end this present inquiry with a comparison of man with one of the higher inferior animals. He would show that the moral nature, as a whole, was much less developed in the highest of these than in man; he would show that love and faith are certainly much less prominent in them; and that hate and fear, though perhaps absolutely less in amount than in man, are, relatively to love and faith, much more developed in the lower animals than in man. If man has descended from a lower form, this would settle the question which we are now considering; for when man began to exist as man, his moral nature would be in an intermediate state between that of the higher animals and that of the lower savages; therefore, since he became man, his moral nature must have altered. But, passing over this argument, let us attempt a comparison between the moral nature of the most advanced races of to-day and the moral nature of, say, the Aryan people of the Ganges in the time of Guatama, of the Greeks toward the end of the fifth century before Christ, and of the Jews from the time of Saul and David to the time of the prophets. And in making these comparisons let us consider, as far as our data will allow us, the attitude of the four fundamental moral functions toward—(1) Husband, wife, father, mother, children; (2) The individual's own nation or race; (3) Mankind at large; (4) Enemies; (5) The lower animals; (6) External nature—as scenery, sun, moon and stars, spring, flowers, and also toward the real or supposed hostile aspects of nature, such as storm, earthquake, eclipse; (7) The unknowable, as shown by the character of the gods which they carved out of it, or with which they peopled it; and (8) Toward death.

I. *Buddhism.*—In a given moral nature of a certain total volume the less faith there is the more fear there is; and the more fear there is the less faith there is. The same is true of love and hate. Now it is certain that there are races of men upon the earth in whom fear preponderates over faith, so that the gods which they imagine to exist are more evil than good, and their supposed condition after death is more to be dreaded than desired. It is equally certain that there are upon the earth now races of men of whom the reverse of this is true, so that the god or gods which they imagine to exist are more good than evil, and their supposed condition after death is more to be desired than dreaded. Now suppose that at a given period of the world's history all men, or all the men of a given nation, were in the former of these conditions, and supposing further that there is such a thing as development of the moral nature, and that the moral nature of this nation was on the whole advancing, then there must come a time when they would reach the line which divides preponderance of faith from preponderance of fear. The moral progress of the world or of a nation is intermittent. It is made, a stride now and a stride again, as the men appear who are capable of initiating advance. A given people might either pause at the neutral line, or step from just below it to just above it. There has occurred at least one case in the world's history in which a large section of the human race has taken its station for a time just on the line indicated. Reaching this line as they did from below, the attainment of it was to them a moral elevation; and not only so, but the highest moral elevation which they were at that time capable of. So that what, to the higher races of to-day, seems so inconceivable, was to them a living, realized fact; and *nirvâna*—annihilation—was their last and best ideal of what the universe had in store for man. This was the step made by Guatama twenty-five hundred years ago in northern Hindustan—a step which has been followed by hundreds of millions of men and women for now twenty-five centuries. Buddhism sprang from its antecedent religion, Brahmanism, which was itself a direct descendant or a continuation of the religion of the Aryan people before their separation and divergence to south and west. I have not been able to find the exact value of this initial religion, but for many reasons I am satisfied that it was lower than Buddhism—that it represented less faith and more fear—that its gods, in the aggregate, were more evil than good, and that the condition anticipated after death, even in the case of the best men, was more to be feared than desired —that, in fact, it was the projection of a moral nature in which fear preponderated over faith. Every new religion derives its authority from, and establishes its hold upon man by, the fact that it represents a moral advance, that it is a projection into the unknown of a superior and more assured hope. This law has no exceptions. In the nature of the case it could not have any; for no people or nation, having attained a certain degree of assurance as to the friendliness to mankind of the governing power of the universe, will willingly follow the man who tells them that it is less friendly than they thought it. But we are all ready to follow the man, if we can, who, having more faith than we have, inspires us with the confidence to believe that the universe is more friendly to us than we supposed. A parallel fact to the birth of Buddhism was the development of Zoroastrianism from the same primitive stock, that is from the initial Aryan faith. This religion seems to have had almost exactly the same moral value as Buddhism, for whereas this last placed its highest hope in *nirvâna*, Zoroastrianism represented the government of the universe to be in the hands of a good and an evil principle, of which neither was stronger than the other. Now, a plus and a minus quantity which are equal to one another are equal to zero ; *nirvâna* is also equal to zero ; so that from our present point of view Buddhism and Zoroastrianism are each, morally considered, equal to zero, and are therefore equal to one another. I need not insist upon the fact that, speaking generally, all the religions which have originated subsequently to Buddhism, and which have been held by the foremost races of men, such as the various forms of Christianity and Mahometanism, all differ from Buddhism and Zoroastrianism in these two essential particulars—first, that they declare the good power or principle in the government of the universe to be stronger than the evil power; and, secondly, that they represent the state beyond the grave to be, for the good man, more to be desired than feared. The meaning of this, of course, is that with advanced nations in modern times, that is, speaking generally, in the last two thousand years, the scale has turned, and faith is now in the human mind in excess of fear, and consequently the ideas projected into the unknown world by man's moral nature, are, on the whole, a plus quantity instead of being, as with the lower races, a minus quantity, or simply equal to zero. I have no data with which to compare the moral nature of the early Buddhists with the moral nature of the modern advanced races, except in this particular of the essential value of the religion possessed by each. I shall, therefore, pass on to the consideration of the moral elevation attained by the Greeks of about the time of Pericles.

II. *Greece.*—The moral nature of the ancient Greeks was characterized by exaltation of love, a proportionate dwarfing of hate, a considerably less development of faith than of love, and a consequent preponderance of fear. The excess of love over faith is shown principally by their extraordinary achievements in the arts on the one hand, and by the low type of their religion on the other. The excess of fear over hate is shown chiefly by the character of their wars, and the incidents springing out of these wars. Let us consider very briefly these four points.

In poetry (not music), sculpture, architecture, oratory, and painting (?), the Greeks of the fifth century before Christ reached, perhaps, as high a level as has been reached in the whole history of the world, and a far higher level than had been reached elsewhere up to that time. Their family affections, as far as we can see, appear to have been well developed. Friendship with them between men not connected by blood seems to have reached a very high point. This last fact is probably largely due to the curious connection which existed with them between friendship and sexual love, by which a certain amount of the latter was carried over to the account of the former. Of their feeling toward animals little is known. They had far less love of nature than the people of modern nations.

Their want of faith is shown in their deficient trust of one another—a want which led to their ruin, for it prevented them from combining. But above all this want is shown by their conceptions of man's state after death, and of the central fact of the universe—that is, of the character of their gods. Their Hades was a gloomy, cheerless realm, the supreme governorship of which was not equal in value to the earthly life of a slave; and their gods, while careful of their own honor and service, were careless of their human worshipers, and while not cruel and revengeful, as are the gods of savages, still visited with fearful punishments very trifling omissions in the rites due to them from men. Such a future world and such gods could only have been created or adopted by a people in whom faith was greatly deficient.

With respect to fear and hate, though the Greeks fought well upon occasion, it was almost invariably when they were cornered and could not help fighting. Thermopylæ is an exception to this rule, and doubtless the Spartans were braver than the Ionic Greeks, that is to say, they had more faith. They also had less love, as shown by their greater selfishness in political matters, and by their want of advance in and appreciation of the arts. So, likewise, hate, showing itself specially in the form of cruelty, was a more prominent moral function with them than with the Ionic Greeks. Their practice of exposing such of their children as they did not think it desirable to bring up, and the atrocious and cold-blooded massacre of the Helots by order of the Ephors, in the eighth year of the Peloponnesian war, are sufficient examples of their notable want of sympathy. At Salamis the voice of a vast majority of the leaders was for retreat, and the Greek fleet would have retreated if Themistokles had not made retreat impossible. The victory of Platæa was due far more to the want of courage of the army of Mardonius than to the possession of this quality by the army of Pausanias, though doubtless parts of this last army did some good fighting. But what should we say now of an army corps, supposed to be exceptionally brave, which should twice, in face of the enemy, arrange with the rest of the army a change of position to avoid meeting the best troops on the side of the enemy? Yet Pausanias and his Spartans did this at Platæa to avoid the Persians, and, strange to say, no one seemed to think it a singular or a cowardly act on their part.

The family affections of the Greeks of the time of Pericles were certainly not more developed than they are with us to-day. They were probably a good deal less developed; the exact difference can hardly, I think, be estimated. Their sympathies, outside their families and immediate friends, were certainly far less intense and less wide-spreading than our own. An average Greek could hardly be said to have any sympathy for people outside his own small state. Outside the Hellenic race he had less than none; that is, he was hostile or antagonistic to all people outside this limit. Such a sentiment as the love of humanity he would have been incapable of understanding; and such feeling as we have for distant suffering, as shown in the case of the Chicago fire, or the late Southern pestilence, would be altogether beyond his widest reach of sympathy.

There is no evidence that the Greeks had any feeling toward the lower animals such as is common among ourselves. But where they fell farther behind us than in any other particular, perhaps, was in the want of the love of nature, a feeling that seems to have been almost entirely absent in them, and which is so prominent in our own mental organization. From all these considerations, as well as from innumerable others which might easily be urged were it necessary, it seems to me certain that with the Greeks of the fifth century before Christ love was, on the whole, somewhat less developed than it is with us, and that faith was a good deal less developed, and that hate was slightly and fear markedly more prominent functions in their minds than they are in ours.

III. *The Jews.*—In the case of the ancient Jews, the first thing to be remarked is that their moral nature differed from that of the Greeks by a markedly greater development of faith and a less development of love, and that therefore hate was more and fear less pronounced with them than with the ancient Greeks. In fact, the great want in the peoples of the Aryan race as compared with the peoples belonging to the Semitic race, and therefore in the religions which the Aryan peoples have created, whether Brahmanism, Buddhism, Zoroastrianism, Magism, Druidism, or the religions of the ancient Greeks or Romans, has always been want of faith. The whole race has always been deficient in this supreme quality. Up to the era of the foundation of Christianity, the Semites were the only people who had created a religion in which the good principle in the government of the universe was clearly dominant over the evil principle. Amongst the Semites the Jews were not alone in having passed the median line so often here indicated. The writer of the Book of Job was not a Jew, and in that great work the supremacy of Jehovah is fully recognized; and not only so, but it is fully recognized that Jehovah's attributes were far more good than evil, though it might be difficult for men to see that they were so. And here it may be well to remark that at the time of the earliest Jewish writings which have come down to us, although Jehovah is fully recognized as the preponderant power in the government of the universe, yet it is doubtful whether his attributes at this early time were not fully as much evil as good, so that at that time it cannot be said that with these people the median line, as we may call it, was passed. We have now seen three modes by which this median line may be represented by the intellect: (1) In the case of Buddhism, by atheism and annihilation; (2) In the case of Zoroastrianism, by good and evil powers of equal strength; (3) In the case of early Judaism, by a god in whose attributes good and evil are equally balanced, toward whom fear and faith go out in equal degrees. In relation to the moral nature, these three conceptions are equal to one another, in other words these three conceptions are inspired by moral natures which have reached the same level. At the time of the writing of the Psalms, however, say by the end of the eleventh century B. C., this line was clearly passed, and the Jews had attained to a moral elevation, viewed from which the government of the universe was seen to be, on the whole, more favorable than the reverse to the children of men. From this time to the era of the foundation of Christianity a more or less steady elevation of the moral nature of the Jews took place, an elevation evidenced by the sublime compositions of the prophets, until the last great step made by this people was taken by Jesus, and men were made to feel, and through their feelings to see, that the old, awful Jehovah, that jealous God, who visited the sins of the fathers upon the children unto the third and fourth generation, was in reality " our Father who art in heaven." The man, through the extraordinary elevation of whose moral nature this advance was made, may well be called divine, for he was and is divine.

Referring now to page 136, let us consider as well as we can the moral nature of the ancient Jews somewhat more in detail, so as to compare it with our own moral nature at the present time. (1.) The family affections of this remarkable people, as far back as we can go, seem to have been well developed. (2.) Their national instinct or their love for the members of their own race seems also to have been well marked from a very early period. (3.) Here, however, their sympathies stop short. Love of humanity was a feeling to which they never attained. They were always ready, in every sense, to spoil the Egyptians, and not only so, but to glory in doing it. They always looked upon the non-Jews as inferior people, and despised them; and they were doubtless right in thinking the Gentiles inferior to themselves, but they were not right in despising them. (4.) They have always been a bitter people to their enemies; no nation above the state of savagery ever made war in a fiercer or more cruel spirit. The massacres which they committed when they got the upper hand were numerous and terrible, and worse than that, they gloried in them. The Jews contrast very unfavorably with the Greeks in regard to cruelties practiced in war. Among the worst acts of the Greeks of this kind were the massacre at Mitylênè, and the massacres at Korkyra. All these seem to me to have been prompted at least as much by fear as by hate, and they do not compare in savagery to any of the numerous massacres recorded in the early books of the Old Testament, and evidently exulted in by those who committed them. (5.) Just what was the state of their feelings to the lower animals I do not know. It is probable that their sympathies in this direction were very limited. It is certain that they had not the same love for the non-human inhabitants of the earth as we have, or something of this feeling must have appeared in their literature. Later in their history the superiority of the moral nature of Jesus to his Jewish predecessors is shown almost as much by his exquisite sense of the beauty and divinity of animated nature and man—that is, by love—as by his splendid trust in the goodness of the governor of the universe—that is, by faith. (6.) They appear to have been destitute of the feeling which we call love of nature, which in the best of us moderns reaches the degree of intense passion. (7.) The God of the Jews from the eleventh to the sixth century B.C. was the highest god which had so far been imagined, but no one will say that this deity was as high a conception as was the God of Jesus, who has been and is the God of the Christians, and therefore, speaking generally, of the moderns. The God of the ancient Jews was less loving, less merciful than is the God of the moderns—that is to say, they had less faith than we have. I know it may be said, and fairly said, that we owe our faith largely to them, but that does not alter the argument. (8.) It does not appear that the ancient Jews believed in immortality; the author of Job (see Renan's translation, p. 56, *et seq.*) discusses the question very fully, and decides against a future life. The author of Ecclesiastes says that which befalleth the sons of men befalleth beasts; one lot befalleth both. As the one dieth, so dieth the other. The ancient Jews did not look with complacency upon death; their best men considered it a thing to fear and dislike—an inevitable misfortune—a blot upon the generally beneficent scheme of the universe. Not so our best men; they make friends with death. If they are Christians they have more or less definite ideas of a future state; and for the good man (and, according to some more advanced sects of Christians, for the bad man also) either at once, or after a period of probation, the state of the dead is supposed to be more desirable than the state of the living. If they are not Christians, they do not pretend to know what the name death means, or what state lies behind that veil—whether the existence beyond will be conscious or unconscious—whether the state will be individual or diffused; but they believe that death is good just as surely as life is good. They know no more about it than the ancient Jews did, but they have more faith. It must not be supposed that I intend to say that even the men who have the most faith at the present time desire their own death because they feel certain that the state after death is more to be desired than feared. There are two reasons why this state of mind will probably never be reached. The first is that the instinctive fear of death, which is quite apart from and independent of religious convictions, and which is a result of natural selection, will, no doubt, though it is declining in strength as the race advances toward mental maturity, always exist in sufficient force to prevent it; and, secondly, because, as our faith toward the unknown advances, so does our faith toward the known also advance. So that as we have more faith toward our state after death, we have more faith toward the things that surround us in life; and not only so, but as faith advances so does love advance, and the man who has the most faith has also the most love; and by the time that the manacles of fear which have so far chiefly held us to this life are loosened, if that time ever comes, love will have woven cords not less strong to withhold us from the brink of that shadowy river which we sometimes long yet tremble to cross. My general conclusion is that the ancient Jews were behind us in faith and still more in love; that fear was a more prominent function, and hate a good deal more prominent function, of their moral nature than of ours. The result, then, of this hasty and cursory inquiry into the mental state of our remote ancestors leads to the conclusion that the moral nature is not a fixed quantity, but that it is altering in the direction of more love and faith and less hate and fear.

In the second place, let us compare the moral nature of savages with that of the more civilized races of men. Most people will admit, whether they believe in evolution or not, that the initial state of man was that of a savage—that the mental constitution savages possess, we, or at least our ancestors once possessed, and nothing more. So that if the moral nature of a savage differs from that of a civilized man, the moral nature cannot be a fixed quantity. How, then, does the moral nature of a savage compare with the moral nature of an average man belonging to one of the advanced nations of Europe or America? The lowest savages are said to possess little love or faith, and to have the functions hate and fear, especially fear, largely developed. Baker (*Albert N' Yanza*) says, " They are universally cowardly, and do not know what love is. They have no idea of gratitude, and think that anything that is done to please them is done because the doer is afraid of them and wishes to propitiate them. Love, even for wife, husband, or child, does not seem to exist among them. Faith they have absolutely none. They have no belief in a god or future state—indeed, laugh at the idea of this last." They hardly get beyond—perhaps do not get beyond—sexual desire. Their love for their offspring and for their father and mother is, perhaps, the strongest feeling of this sort that they possess, and their affection for their near relations is not strong as compared with ours; for many savages will sell their children for a moderate consideration, and many kill and desert their parents when they become old and helpless. Every man outside a very limited circle is an enemy to the savage. He has, to say the best of it, no good feeling for any one beyond this narrow limit. His feeling toward his gods, when he has any, is a mixture of hate and fear. This is certain from the account he himself gives of these imaginary beings. Death he regards with intense and unmixed terror. "Most of the Finnish and Altaic tribes," says Castren, "cherish a belief that death, which they look upon with terrible fear, does not entirely destroy individual existence." The aspects of nature have no moral significance for him except in a bad sense. Storm, tempest, night, earthquakes, eclipses, and all the darker phenomena of earth and air fill him with vague fear, which is often intense. On the other hand, the brighter aspects of nature, from which we derive such a large proportion of our happiness, awaken in him no enthusiasm. Sunshine, flowers, glancing rivers, lake expanses, and all that to us in nature is so beautiful, is not beautiful to him. If the aspects of nature are favorable to his pursuit of food, he is satisfied, no more. If they are adverse to him, he is cast down. If they are unusual, he is terrified. Terror, indeed, is the most prominent of the moral functions in the mind of the savage. Reade (*Martyrdom of Man*) says: "It is impossible to describe or even to imagine the tremulous condition of the savage mind; yet the traveler can see from their aspect and manner that they dwell in a state of never-ceasing dread." Sir J. Lubbock (*Prehistoric Times*) says: "It is not too much to say that the horrible dread of unknown evil hangs like a thick cloud over savage life, and embitters every pleasure." What I say of the moral nature of savages is true in broad outline of all savages, whatever their color and whatever their race. Quotations similar to the above might easily be extended indefinitely; but those given are sufficient to establish what few would think of denying—the fact that the moral nature of savages is lower than the moral nature of civilized man. We cannot deny this. We must admit a difference, and at the bottom the difference is this: in the savage mind there is absolutely and relatively less love and less faith; and certainly, relatively, and perhaps absolutely, more hate and more fear.

Now, what shall we say of the moral nature of children as compared with the moral nature of grown-up people of the same race? In the first place, their capacity for affection is certainly very limited. This is perhaps best shown by the absence of grief for the loss of those by death whom they would love if they loved anybody. Children up to eight years old rarely grieve to any marked degree upon the death of father, mother, sister, or brother. Many young children have a way of seeming very affectionate, and our affection for

7*

them misleads us, and makes us think that they love us as we love them. Not only is it capable of proof that young children are not susceptible of love to any great degree, but it is certain that boys and girls almost grown up are greatly deficient as compared with mature men and women in this faculty. A remarkably shrewd old lady once said to the author that from her observation upon herself and others—and her opportunities for observation had been ample—she was satisfied that young girls were almost absolutely heartless. The Germans have an emphatic mode of expressing the same thing. With them all the names for girl, as—*mädchen, mädlein, fräulein*, except *magd* and *dirne*, which two have not exactly the meaning of our word girl, are neuter; but no one pretends that the faculty of loving, any more than any other faculty or organ, comes into existence all at once; so that if it be granted, as it must be, that this faculty is absent in quite young children, and as it is only developed gradually, it must be immature still in boys and girls. Faith is equally absent in young children, and equally deficient in youth. Comte remarks that the religion of the young children of the higher races is fetichism, of older children polytheism, and only becomes monotheistic toward puberty. I do not feel sure of the truth of this statement taken literally, but the spirit of the observation is certainly just. No young child—I believe I might say no boy or girl—trusts God as older people often come to do. Children are deficient in confidence and courage, other aspects of faith. They are distrustful, suspicious, cowardly, as compared with grown-up people, and they especially dread and distrust the unknown. Conversely, anger, or dislike, and fear are early developed out of all proportion to their opposites. I fancy that most people who are not too old to look back into their childhood can remember that they felt both fear and hate long before they felt either grief or love. Observation of our own and other people's children will teach us the same fact. Perhaps no one has a better chance of making these observations than a practitioner of medicine. He has first-rate opportunities of observing the capacity of young children to feel terror, and he has better opportunities than most people to observe their anger. Love and faith, then, are developed comparatively late in life; hate and fear comparatively early. Children who are born to die young, tubercular children especially, often spring up mentally to an immature imitation of maturity, like plants chance-sown late in the year, which put out flowers before they are half grown, and press forward in a desperate attempt to mature their fruit, when they have not time to attain to half the normal size of their species. Such children are caught at by tract writers and sensational novelists, and held up as examples by pious people for healthy boys and girls. As well show the six-weeks-old pumpkin on the first of July, covering yards of ground with its immense leaves and vines, and just thinking about flowering, the month-old pumpkin of the first of October, with its miserable fruit already formed, and say : See! take pattern by this pumpkin, you idle plant, who think of nothing but rank growth, and have no care for the duties of life. Do you not see that this plant, younger than you, is already bringing forth fruit? But the idle and rank pumpkin is a valuable plant, and its more forward neighbor is good for nothing.

I have now examined the question, Is the moral nature a fixed quantity? in the three modes by which alone, as far as I know, it can be examined, and the examination by each mode has led to the same conclusion. That conclusion is that the moral nature is not a fixed quantity, but that its two antagonistic halves, love and faith, and hate and fear, are not developed synchronously, but that fear and hate are developed earliest, faith and love later ; that these two last have, and have necessarily, as they grew, encroached upon the two first, until the moral nature of man has become such as we know it to be to-day—not very high, certainly, but still high as compared with its initial state. The next thing for us to consider is the means by which this advance has been effected.

CHAPTER V

THE HISTORY OF THE DEVELOPMENT OF THE MORAL NATURE.

"The Lord advances, and yet advances;
Always the shadow in front; always the reached hand, bringing up the laggards."—WALT WHITMAN.

"Peut-être parmi tous les chemins qui suivent les hommes, y on a-t-il un plus grand nombre qu'on n'a coutume de le croire qui débouchent dans le ciel."—MAURICE DE GUÉRIN.

THE problem before us now is, given an average moral nature, in which hate and fear greatly preponderate over love and faith, to find by what means hate and fear were caused gradually to lessen, and love and faith gradually to increase, until the level of the present average moral nature was reached.

These means have been—(I.) Natural Selection; (II.) Sexual Selection; (III.) Social Life; (IV.) Art; (V.) Religion.

I. *Natural Selection.*—We have seen (pp. 75, *et seq.*) that elevation of the moral nature is intimately associated, through the relation of the moral nature to the great sympathetic nervous system, with physical and mental vigor, with health and length of life, and we know that elevation of the moral nature is as surely inherited as any other mental or bodily possession. This being so, it is easy to see that those nations, tribes, families, or individuals in whom this moral elevation exists must have an advantage over those in whom it does not exist in the same degree. Moreover, as intellectual superiority on the whole (p. 80) goes along with moral elevation, this gives those endowed with the last another very great advantage over those who are endowed with it in less proportion. The men, then, who have this master quality, moral elevation, in the fullest development, will certainly have on an average more children (p. 84, *et seq.*), and will have more health, strength, wisdom, and courage, and a longer life with which to rear, protect, and provide for these children; which children, themselves inheriting this superior moral nature, will prosper more than the average of men and women of their age and country, and transmit, in their turn, the advantage which they inherited to their posterity. Such superior individuals and races must necessarily encroach upon the inferior individuals and races with whom they come into competition in the struggle for existence, and eventually supplant these last—a process which is said to be taking place at the present time in Europe in the case of the Jews, who, it is said, are increasing in numbers much more rapidly than the populations among which they live, and who are certainly attracting to themselves far more than their share, according to number, of the wealth of these countries, and therefore more of the comforts and conveniences of life. As to the superiority of the moral nature of the Jews as a race, I think there can be no question about it (p. 76, *et seq.*, and p. 144, *et seq.*). By the process above indicated, a steady upward tendency is secured, as long as the primal energy which originated the human race shall continue unexhausted within it. It may be said further, that elevation of the moral nature protects those who possess it, other things being equal, from sensual habits and vices; and thus besides being, as it is in the first place, an accompaniment of health and strength, becomes also a cause of these.

II. *Sexual Selection.*—The greater the power of loving in men and women, the greater, other things being equal, will be the inclination to marry; and, on the other hand, nothing attracts men and women so much as love in the opposite sex. On the whole, therefore, individuals with the faculty of loving strongly developed will be more sure to marry and have descendants than other individuals with the faculty of loving less developed. By means of natural selection and sexual selection, therefore, the families and races with a higher moral nature tend to encroach upon and extinguish families and races with a lower moral nature, and so to retain and diffuse the highest moral elevation which has been reached at any given time. From this highest moral plateau spring up from time to time—in accordance with the law that the offspring, while resembling the parents, differ from them also—still higher moral natures. These in their turn tend to be preserved and diffused as before. These two means to the great end are real and operative, but the process of moral perfectionment, slow as it is, would be infinitely slower if these means alone had to be depended upon.

III. *Social Life.*—Each child begins life without a moral nature, but with a certain inherited faculty of developing a more or less elevated moral nature in accordance with the child's antecedents and in accordance with the medium in which the mind of the child expands. After a few years the child has a moral nature, but of a much lower order, in civilized countries at least, than that possessed by the adults among whom it lives. The child, if brought up among savages, or cut off altogether from human society like the children in the experiment of Psammetichus, would acquire a moral nature which, however, would be undoubtedly of a very low order. This aborted moral nature the child would derive directly by heredity from its parents. In social life the next step beyond this initial hereditary condition of the moral nature is made through contact with father, mother, brothers, sisters, and other members of the household. The child absorbs love chiefly from its mother, and faith chiefly from its father. How? By contact with their moral natures. Yes, but how by contact? Pygmalion, by intense love, infused love—that is, life—into his statue. The love of the mother permeates the child. The faith of the father permeates the child. How does this happen? I do not think we can tell, but it does happen. We see the same thing taking place on a larger scale in the spread of emotion through a body of men, as in the case of a panic in an army or city; or as in the case of the divine *phêmê* which flew into and spread through the Grecian camp on the fourth of the month Boêdromion, immediately before the battle of Mykale, which occurrence, along with many other things, proved to Herodotus that the gods take part in the affairs of man; or, as in the case of religious enthusiasm, that is love and faith, at a camp meeting or revival. For what is called "getting religion" is not a fancy. It is as genuine an experience as "falling in love," and is a somewhat parallel phenomenon to this last. It consists in an elevation of the whole moral nature, both love and faith, rapidly affected, usually, perhaps always, by contact with another moral nature previously in this elevated state. It is a genuine exaltation of the subject of it at the time—the discredit thrown upon it being due to the fact that this exalted state is apt to be temporary, and the future life of the person fail to justify the expectations which he or she excite during the period of moral elevation. These waves of feeling are not dependent upon ideas, and this ebb and flow of feeling, without the intervention of ideas, is not confined to instances on the great scale such as those given, but is taking place every day and all day long whenever there are several people together, and may be verified by any one who has a tolerably sensitive moral nature a dozen times a day if he or she will only pay attention to it. The following is an extreme instance of what I am now speaking about. I once attended a lady who died under peculiarly painful circumstances. A few minutes after her death I met her husband in another room. He had been summoned on account of her critical condition. He said "How is ——?" I said, "It is all over." He said, "Dead?" These were the only words spoken by either of us. His face showed very little sign of emotion. The moment he spoke, or even, I think, before he spoke the one word "Dead?" I felt an intense vibration or thrill of grief sweep through my body. Instantly the tears literally poured from my eyes. All this during the moment while I still stood looking at him. Almost at the same instant tears ran from his eyes in a stream, and directly afterward blood poured rapidly from both his nostrils. This man, who was about twenty-five years old, and in excellent health, died in about three months after this of a broken heart. Now in this case there can be no question as to the intensity of feeling on the part of the person in whom it was initiated. There is equally little doubt in my mind as to the direct overflow in this case of feeling from the one moral nature to the other, independently of the intellect. For I had no means of knowing the intensity of his feeling, and still I felt it. I have seen a good many men lose their wives, and a good many women lose their husbands, both before and since that time. I have seen emotion expressed in every way, I think, that it can be expressed. I have never been affected by it myself in the same manner nor to the same degree. And subsequent events showed to my satisfaction that I have never, before or since, stood in the presence of such intense grief as on that occasion.

The child feels the love of its mother who is bending over it while it is asleep, though it is not conscious of it, just as the seed feels the sun's rays, though it is an inch under the ground, and is unconscious of the existence of a sun or of anything else. The boy feels the courage—that is, faith—of his father, as he walks with him through dark woods or wild strange places. Any one who has been at sea in a dangerous storm, and who has at all observed his own feelings, knows how differently he felt when in company with one or two of the ship's officers who had no fear, and when he was with some of the passengers who were greatly alarmed.

In this way, by contact more or less close in social life, the mass of the work is done ;—by short steps—in the common associations of every day, in every household—always—among children, young men, young women—among the average people. The superior moral nature of the household, the village, the city, the state, the country, takes the lead and the rest follow—closer or farther off they follow—whether with willing or reluctant steps they follow—slower or faster they follow; and in front of the leaders is a solid wall of blackness, into which they are marching, though into which they cannot see. I say the foremost leads and the rest follow. Who is the foremost? He or she with the most love or faith, or both; and consequently with the least hate or fear, or both. In the typical household, and in all good households, there is an approximation to the ideal society. The mother leads in love, the father in faith; and from them, by contact with them, the children catch this love and faith, and it is gradually transferred to them without being lost to the parents. "For if you divide pleasure and love, each part exceeds the whole, and we know not how much, while any yet remains unshared, of pleasure may be gained. This truth is that deep well whence sages draw the unenvied light of hope."

Does not the love of a mother make the child love? If not, what is it good for? And what does make the child love? Does not the courage, the faith of the father to face whatever exists or may happen in this world or the next, give courage or faith to the children who are with him every day, and whose greatest ambition is to emulate their father, who to them is the greatest of heroes, as their mother is the chief of saints? If it does not, whence do they get their courage, their faith? Does not the love and faith—the absence of hate and fear—in the good priest, warm and strengthen the heart and elevate the life of his congregation? If not, what is the good of him? We know that mothers and fathers and priests often fail, from want of the qualities in question in themselves, to fill, from a moral point of view, the place they occupy in the social scheme—fail to vivify the souls entrusted to their care—to feed the souls which depend on them for spiritual food, and which, unsupplied by them, are starved and undeveloped. We know that women are mothers who never should have been mothers, as far as we can see; that men are fathers who never should have been fathers; and that—more inexcusable still, and more common—men are priests who never should have been priests. What then? The child gets another spiritual father, mother, leader, such as he can get, good or bad, and fares, spiritually, well or ill, as he can. To the higher grades of moral natures those in the lower ranks all occupy the position of children. The lower as well as the higher are all capable of more or less exaltation if subjected to the proper influence, both child, and man, and woman.

It would not be right to leave out of sight entirely that agent in moral advance which has so far been generally considered the sole agent. I refer to excitation of the moral nature through and by the intellect. I have purposely kept this mode of acting upon the moral nature in the background because I believe—in fact, I know—it deserves very little of the weight which has usually been attached to it. It is true that the intellect may serve as a channel for the conveyance of emotion; but alterations in the moral nature can never have their source in the intellect either of the person experiencing the emotion or of any one else. The person who seeks to act upon the moral nature of another must himself feel the emotion he wishes to excite; then his own intellect and the intellect of the person to be acted upon may be used as a channel to convey from the one moral nature to the other the moral state in question; but this is the only way, or almost the only way, in which the intellect comes into action in the evolution of moral states. The notion that grown-up people or children are made better by rules and catechisms cannot be too soon done away with.

IV. *Art.*—Here and there, on the face of the earth, in the course of the ages, are born men whose moral natures are superior to those of their contemporaries, as there are others born whose intellects are more keen and piercing. These men we call poets, artists, orators; they are the high priests of humanity. The essential feature which distinguishes these men from the men about them is that they love more and have more faith than these. They love more intensely. They love more objects. Their love reaches a higher level and covers more surface than in the case of the average man. And they have more faith—more trust in God and nature—more confidence in the essential goodness of men, women, and themselves. They necessarily, therefore, hate less and fear less. If the elevated moral nature of these men died with them, their existence would be comparatively valueless to mankind. By natural selection and sexual selection they would undoubtedly exert a certain influence upon the race which in tens of thousands of years would become appreciable. The moral nature of all men, however, possesses this quality—that it can be acted upon, moved, elevated; and there is a mysterious relation, a sympathy, existing among men by which we are all compelled, in spite of ourselves, to seek to impress our influence, whether for good or evil, upon one another. Under the operation of this law, the men of superior moral natures have sought for and found various means by which they might convey to others their moral attitude toward themselves and their surroundings. These means we call by the generic name of art. The principal divisions of art are poetry, oratory, music, painting, sculpture, architecture. By all these means men express moral states with more or less clearness and fullness. In some instances they express ideas as well as moral states; but just to the extent that, or in the degree that, the production is a work of art, the moral state is the central matter to be expressed, and the ideas are simply used to assist in this object. In poetry, oratory, painting, and sculpture, ideas are used in this way or expressed incidentally. In music, no ideas are expressed along with the moral state, and if any ideas are excited by a symphony or sonata, they are excited by the moral state and are secondary to it.

Now, suppose a man is born into the world with a moral nature greatly superior to the average moral natures of the men about him; it does not necessarily follow that his intellect should be very much above, or even that it should be at all above, the average, but it is very likely that it will be, for the reasons given at p. 80, and a certain intellectual superiority must accompany the moral elevation to enable the man to find expression for this last.

An elevated moral nature is one in which love or faith or both are in excess, and hate or fear, or both, are consequently in diminished amount. How will such a moral nature act in art, or by means of art, on the men who surround and succeed it so as to raise their moral natures? And here we must notice that all that is really required is contact. Let a lower moral nature come into contact with a higher moral nature, and the first will be improved, that is elevated, by the last. What the artist has to do, therefore, is to project his moral nature, by means of sounds, colors, forms, or ideas, so that other moral natures may come in contact with it, either through the senses or through the intellect.

Let us suppose that the artist to be considered is a poet. His moral elevation will probably consist chiefly in excess of love with a proportionate extinction of its opposite, hate. But, as we have seen, the other positive function of the moral nature, faith, will be in him almost certainly above the average, and may even be in excess of love. A poet must have a certain elevation of faith as well as of love, or he becomes contemptible from what we call weakness.

Men in whose moral natures faith is greatly in excess of love, both functions being very prominent, or men in whom both love and faith are extraordinarily developed, scarcely use poetry as a mode of expression; it is inadequate to their purpose. These men will be considered farther on.

There are many poets who, with a certain moral elevation, depend more in their compositions on an acute intellect than upon the direct inspiration of the heart. This class of poets is often greatly admired by their contemporaries, but they make no impression upon the great heart of humanity, and their works soon die.

The love of the poet, as all love, is principally expended in associations with ideas of known things—such as men, women, children, animals, flowers, the aspects of nature—in short, all natural objects. In other words, the function of the poet has always been to exalt the "beloved brotherhood of earth, ocean, and air, and their great mother, nature," and to create for our admiration the most heroic men and the most beautiful and tender-hearted women. Toward such things as excite hate in others, the better moral nature of the poet is shown by absence or lessening of that hate. So that in such a moral nature the things loved by an average moral nature are loved more: the things neither loved nor hated by an average moral nature are loved; the objects that are disliked by the average moral nature are liked or are indifferent to this moral nature; and the things that are hated by the average moral nature are hated not at all or less by the higher moral nature supposed. This must be understood not literally but generally, and as being not specifically but essentially true. In applying this generalization to actual men, allowance would have to be made for character—that is to say, the difference in different people of the adhesions between concepts and moral states (p. 34). Given, then, such a moral nature, in which love is largely developed, and hate proportionately dwarfed—in which faith is well developed and fear below the average, and along with this a good intellect, and you have the raw material of an artist in words, tones, colors, or forms. We will say that the man becomes an artist—that he becomes a poet; many things go to decide whether this happens or not, but we will say it happens, then what does he do? What is the manner of his work? His work is to associate intellectual images with a higher level of moral feeling than had before been associated with those images, and to this end he expresses by language both the intellectual concept and the higher moral state bound together, so that they can be and are taken up by other minds, thus planting in these other minds the higher moral state and the improved association—in other words, raising the moral nature of the person who receives the impress from the superior mind of the poet. Now, there are two modes which the poet may adopt to effect this object. The first corresponds closely with the method of the religious innovator, and consists in magnifying, under the influence of the emotion to be expressed, the merit of the subject treated, whether this be hero, heroine, mountain view, flower, or whatever it may be, so as to entitle it, as it were, to the association with it of a higher moral state. The second and most truly artistic method is to create or excite in the mind of the reader or hearer, by the music of the words used, and by their connotations, both the connotations of individual words and of series of words arranged in a certain order, the higher moral state which is present in the mind of the poet, and in which the ideas called up by the words are bathed, and with which the concepts so suggested become associated. Of course, the effect of the moral elevation is not limited to the improved association with the ideas suggested by the poem; all other ideas which pass through the mind while the moral exaltation lasts participate in the benefit of the exaltation, so that no one can pass under the influence of a great artist without having his emotions toward his entire surroundings improved. The first of the two methods above indicated may be compared to climbing up a ladder; the second to being floated up by a rising tide. It is not usual for the poet to employ either of these two methods alone; they are generally used together; but sometimes one and sometimes the other has most prominence. If we want to see them used separately—and in this way we shall best realize the essential difference of the two methods, and the essence of each—we must pass outside of poetry proper, and on each side of it we shall see, on the one side one, and on the other side the other, method used, to the exclusion of its fellow. On the one side of poetry stand the prose works intended to appeal to the emotions and passions—that is, to the moral nature—novels, romances, tales, and stories. On the other side stands music. It easy to see that poetry partakes of the methods of these two widely distinct modes of acting upon the moral nature. It has the idea-suggesting power of the one mode through its words; and it has part of the power of affecting the moral nature directly, possessed by the other in virtue of its rhythm, melody, and harmony.

From all the other arts, and indeed from all the other modes of communication between individuals, music stands apart as being the only mode by which one moral nature can at will hold intercourse with another without the intervention, more or less declared, of the intellect. It is also the means by which the fullest transference of moral states can be obtained; that is, a larger range of moral states can be communicated from mind to mind by music than in any other way, and probably the individual states can be conveyed more accurately. This being so, it is undoubted that music is destined to play in the future of our race a most important part in the development of man's moral nature, probably a more important part than any other single agent. Music appeals to the sense of hearing, and through this sense (p. 103, *et seq.*) to the moral nature. The composer must draw his inspiration from moral elevation. The performer and listener may depend largely, or perhaps even altogether, for their skill and pleasure upon the sense relation, and may be very skillful in the one case, and enjoy great pleasure in the other case, and still not have in either case an elevated moral nature. In this sense a close parallel may be drawn between music and sexual intercourse, using this expression in its largest sense. Men value women, and women value men, for the pleasure or for the happiness their society gives (p. 41, *et seq.*). As they place the first of these above the second they descend toward the brutes. As in their every-day life the second ranks over the first, they ascend toward the angels, who neither marry nor are given in marriage, but who, we may suppose, love one another better than we can love one another. That great musicians have, as a matter of fact and observation, aside from any theory, higher moral natures than the average of the people among whom they live, the biographies of these men is sufficient evidence to me. The same remark applies to poets and artists generally; but in measuring the moral elevation of any artist or any man by the records remaining of his life, or by observation of the life itself, it must never be lost sight of that a man with a high moral nature and a good man in the conventional sense are not necessarily by any means synonymous terms. I have repeated sufficiently often what I mean by a man with a high moral nature. Now, by the majority of people a man is called good in proportion as he loves, trusts, hates, or fears in certain orthodox directions—that is, in proportion as his love, faith, hate, and fear are associated

8*

with proper or improper (*i. e.*, usual or unusual, expedient or inexpedient) concepts. If a man bestows all the love he has upon his family, friends, and estate; all the faith he has upon the current religious conceptions and such stocks as are recognized as being safe; if his hate is expended upon personal, business, political, and other opponents, toward whom he exercises an antagonism supposed to be legitimate; and his fear upon such things as others are also afraid of— such a man, I say, may have a very limited stock of love and faith, and a liberal allowance of hate and fear, and still may pass through the world regarded as a good man; while another man, with incomparably more love and faith, and far less hate and fear—such a man as Shelley, for instance—will be considered immoral and irreligious. Let the test be applied as it ought to be applied, and it will be found that all artists, and especially all great artists, have high moral natures. And consider the matter impartially, and the conclusion will be reached that upon this fact and upon nothing else does their charm and their influence depend. The obverse of this is seen in the case of men with exceptionally low moral natures—habitual criminals. It is said of these people, by those who have had the most extensive observation of them, that they are without exception destitute of æsthetic talent, as well as being without moral sense, though many of them have intellects up to or above the average.

V. *Religion.*—Much fewer in number and more thinly distributed over the face of the earth and through the centuries than are the great artists is another class of men superior to them and differing from them in the proportion of the elements which make up their moral nature. These are the religious founders and innovators. The essential fact in the mental constitution of this class of men is that faith in them is preëminently developed; love is almost necessarily nearly equally or equally prominent; and according to the principle before laid down, the intellectual nature is above the average, and will most likely be of a very high order. In considering these men as religious founders or innovators, the central fact to be considered is their mental attitude toward the unknown world. Such a man comes into the world with a moral nature which is in advance, perhaps largely in advance, of the moral natures of all his contemporaries in his feeling of trust and confidence toward the unknown. He feels that the unknown is more favorable to man than it has ever been felt to be before. He cannot rest in this abstract feeling; nor could he communicate it in this abstract form—or rather want of form—for a pure feeling has no form. He, therefore, gives it form by means of his intellectual nature—that is, he shifts his intellectual attitude to make it correspond with his moral attitude, and conveys to others his improved feeling toward the great unknown by giving a different account of that great unknown from that received up to his time (p. 23 *et seq.*). If, for instance, it was said up to his time that there was a multitude of gods, each of whom was limited in his power by the rest, and all of whom were rather doubtful, or more than doubtful, as to their good will toward men, he says, as Mahomet did, that there is one God infinitely powerful and just. Or, if the old belief was already monotheistic, he will perhaps substitute the Christian God for the Jewish God; and we have all some idea what an enormous advance that was—one of the greatest which was ever made in any field by one man. So great, indeed, that the man by whom it was made is still considered by many millions of men belonging to the most advanced races to have been more than human. No one will pretend, I think, that this advance was made by an intellectual effort. It could not have been. No intellect that we can conceive could touch the problem. Neither is there any evidence to show that the man by whom it was made was extraordinarily great by his intellect.

Neither, again, can it be shown, that the substitution was an intellectual advance. It is as reasonable to believe in the Jewish God as in the Christian God. I do not mean the Christian God as conceived at present; but as God was conceived and portrayed by Jesus. The Christian God, as conceived at present, is, I think, a less reasonable conception than the Jewish God. If, then, this substitution was not effected by an intellectual effort—and it was not—it must have been effected by a moral effort; and this is undoubtedly the mode by which it was actually accomplished. In Jesus, faith reached a level which it had never touched before in any human being. He had more trust in the unknown and more confidence in the human race than any one ever had before his time. Having the wonderful trust in the unknown which he did have, he substituted for an infinitely powerful, just, unrelenting, and though loving, yet jealous God, "our Father who art in heaven." The difference is sufficiently marked—the advance, from a moral point of view, unmistakable. In making it, the change of moral attitude was, beyond all question, the initial change. The shifting of the intellectual conception was the means unconsciously taken to express the advanced moral position. As the intellectual conceptions by which faith toward the unknown is interpreted are purely factitious—are useful and truthful solely as an interpretation of faith, and have no objective value at all; and as alterations in the amount of faith can only be expressed in terms of the intellect by giving a different account of the unknown; so this method used in this field has the fullest justification. It has the justification of necessity. The same method, however, has been from the earliest times extensively employed to express a shifting of the moral attitude toward the known; and here it is not justified, or at all events not in anything like the same absolute manner. As Jesus was supreme in faith, fear seems to have been almost absent from his nature; and as he was almost, if not quite, as supreme in love as he was in faith, hate was reduced in him to a minimum; but while there is no positive evidence in the very imperfect and fragmentary account of his life which has come down to us, of his ever having been under the influence of fear, there is some evidence of his having been several times angry. Why did not the Jews adopt the undoubted advance which Jesus made? There were two main reasons why they did not. The first is, that from their peculiarly isolated position among the peoples about them, and from the long duration of their traditions, the Jews differ from all other races in this—that the adhesions between moral states and intellectual concepts are more close in their mental organization than they are in that of any other branch of the human family. In the second place, the moral advance made by Jesus, though, as said above, really very great, was not nearly so striking from their comparatively elevated moral standpoint (p. 144 *et seq.*) as it was from the standpoint of the average Greek, Italian, Macedonian, or Syrian. In point of fact, only one Jew, as far as we know, who appears to have held the religious convictions of his age and country with the usual firmness of the cultivated Jew, was converted to Christianity, and this conversion, we are told, required a miracle to effect it. So, too, in what would be a parallel though not such an extreme case, it may be strongly suspected that, should a man appear to-day with a moral nature bearing the same relation to that of the ordinary orthodox Christian which the moral nature of Jesus bore to that of the ordinary orthodox Jew, he would make no converts among orthodox Christians. They would reject him almost as indignantly as the Jews rejected Jesus.

From our present point of view the step made by Jesus is seen to be, instead of a step from an initial condition to a final condition, merely one step in an immense, perhaps infinite, series, the step itself having been really a long one, but seeming much greater to us in proportion to other similar steps in the same series than it actually was, from our relation to it. Of this series most of the early steps are buried in the obscurity of the past, and those which are to come in the darkness of the future.

A moral nature like that of Jesus, standing high above the moral natures surrounding it, transmits its influence by awakening faith and love in the men and women with whom it comes in contact. They pass on the influence in their turn, unintentionally, often unconsciously, to their contemporaries and successors. The same moral level becomes registered by the aid of the intellect in words, as in the gospels; and thus the good seed grows, reproduces its kind, and grows again. I am satisfied that the intellect, so far from playing the chief part, as generally supposed, in this moral advance, has scarcely anything, perhaps nothing, to do with it. That is, man's moral nature is not improved, as a general thing, by doctrines got from books or from living teachers; or, when this does happen, the moral advance made is always due, not to the doctrine, but to contact with a superior moral nature. The moral nature is undoubtedly influenced by the perusal of books, but not, or not much, by the ideas contained in them. We must always recollect that, in almost every book, except a dictionary or a work on mathematics, we come into contact in reading it with the moral nature of the writer as well as with his intellectual nature, and it is this moral contact which influences our moral nature, and not the intellectual contact.

The Scribes and Pharisees, that is the leading men of his nation, rejected Jesus and the moral advance which he made. The members of the tribe of Koreish, that is the leading men of his nation, rejected Mahomet and the undoubted moral advance which he made. The Brahmans, that is the leading people of his nation, rejected Siddhartha Guatama and the probably great moral advance which he made. This is not accident. It has always been so, and will always be so. Such men as these are never appreciated until they themselves elevate the moral nature of those who receive and transmit their initiative up to that point from which their own moral elevation can be clearly seen; and these instances may teach us this lesson among others—that, although as an abstract proposition, all must admit that it is elevation of the moral nature which at the bottom makes a good man, yet that men are not thought good by their contemporaries in proportion as their moral natures are elevated. Another element in the man's nature, though really much less important, has greater weight than this has in deciding the judgment of the world, and that is the associations which exist between the elements of the moral and intellectual natures. For, let love be developed in a given man to a degree far above the average, and let it be expended, as it must be in that case, upon objects which the average of men think worthless, and the possessor and bestower of this love receives no credit for it, except from the comparatively few people among those who surround him whom his love stimulates to love again; he is probably said, in the way of reproach, to be a friend of publicans and sinners. Or let faith be so far exalted as necessarily to break loose from its anterior intellectual associations, and to interpret itself intellectually afresh, and the man is inevitably considered by those who surround him, as was Jesus by the Pharisees, Socrates by the Athenians, and Spinosa and Shelley by the men about them, to be an atheist. The highest moral level which the average man can understand and appreciate, is that measure of love and faith which fills and warms into fresh life the intellectual conceptions with which these feelings are associated at the time when, and in the country where, the man lives. If love and faith go beyond this, and overflow the old conceptions, then well for mankind, indeed; but generally not well, in the worldly sense, for the subject of the exalted moral nature.

It will probably be thought that in the history of

the development of the moral nature something should be said of the origin and growth of such virtues as honesty, truth, adhesion to principle, fidelity to duty, justice, and chastity. But if what has been said in this essay has not failed in its intention, if the author has at all succeeded in expressing what was in his mind when he wrote it, then it will be clear to the reader that these virtues, and all others, have been treated of either in their elements or by implication; for example, honesty is the mode of action expressive of love and faith, for no man will act dishonestly toward his neighbor if he loves him, and trusts God— *i.e.*, right or goodness. So truth is the mode of speech, expressive in the same way of love and faith. Adherence to principle is an element of character, and not a direct moral quality. The same may be said of fidelity to duty, except in cases where this comes under the head of honesty. Justice is simply honesty; and chastity is, like adherence to principle, an element of character—that is, it arises from and depends upon the strength and continuance of certain bonds between a moral function and an intellectual concept. All men worth anything love some woman, either ideal or real; so all women worth anything love some man, either ideal or real. It is the strength and continuance of the bond between the moral state love and this concept carried into practical life which constitutes chastity. These examples will serve to show that if the fundamental elements of the moral nature are adequately treated, the whole field of morality, though many of the virtues may not be named, is really covered.

We have seen, then, in this chapter and the last, that in the course of the ages from savagery to civilization, love has slowly but surely broadened and deepened in the heart of man from a mere feeble glimmer in our remote ancestors to what we see it to-day. Arising, as it undoubtedly did, in the sexual and parental instincts, it spread to the family, the gens, the phratry, the tribe, the nation, until almost within the memory of living men the love of humanity was born. At the same time it has extended to animal life and to inanimate nature; and while it has broadened, it has equally deepened; for what is the love of a savage for his wife, children, or friends, compared to that of one of ourselves? And as love has broadened and deepened, so has faith. In the same ratio hate and fear have been contracted. It remains now for me to point out the reason of this change in man's moral nature. It is for this that I have written this essay, and if I do not greatly err this reason is well worth the consideration of every one of us.

CHAPTER VI.

THE INFERENCE TO BE DRAWN FROM THE DEVELOPMENT OF THE MORAL NATURE AS TO THE ESSENTIAL FACT OF THE UNIVERSE.

"I swear the earth shall surely be complete to him or her who shall be complete!
I swear the earth remains jagged and broken only to him or her who remains jagged and broken!"

WALT WHITMAN.

SUPPOSING there is such an advance in the moral nature as is here claimed; that hate and fear are dying out, and that love and faith are becoming more and more developed, what inference can we draw from this fact? In the first place, we may say with confidence that this moral development has not reached its limit, and that it will continue in the future in essentially the same direction that it has pursued in the past. So that there must come a time when, should the race of men endure long enough, the moral functions of fear and hate, with their compounds, which of course depend on them, will be almost or quite extinct, like rudimentary organs in the higher vertebrata which linger long imperfectly formed after the animal has outgrown the need of them and at last fade away entirely. And the moral functions of love and faith, with their compounds, will be as much in advance of these same functions in the best men and women of to-day as those of to-day are in advance of the corresponding functions in the cave-dweller of thirty or forty thousand years ago, or of his prototype the Bushman or Australian of to-day. The question then arises, which moral nature corresponds to—is <u>justified</u> by—the fact of the universe? That of a Bushman? That of the superior man or woman of to-day? That of the man as far in advance of the superior man or woman of to-day as he or she is in advance of the Bushman? Or none of these? Let us consider this a moment. Man's active nature has developed in the past, is developing to-day, and every one supposes it will develop in the future. Why, and how? It seems that it develops because man's active nature can only grow or expand by becoming more and more in accord with the modes of existence of force in the external world; and because man's active nature, like all other functions and organs, is forced, in accordance with the universal law of evolution, to expand or develop. Man's active nature is, in fact, becoming, by contact with it, and as it were by pressure upon it, moulded upon the external world; for by means of his active nature man places himself in what seem to him, and are, in fact, more and more advantageous positions toward the external universe. He is becoming modified into more complete adaptation to this. He invents mechanisms of various sorts, which may be looked upon as extensions of his active nature. He trains himself to do thousands of things which it would once have seemed to him impossible ever to have achieved, and which things are advantageous to him in many ways—such as protecting him from heat, cold, wet, hunger, from wild beasts and enemies; which are useful to him in attacking enemies; in procuring, accumulating, and distributing the means of subsistence; in intercommunication; in facilities of movement from place to place. We all know that man, in his active life, continually brings himself more and more into harmony with the active forces of nature. The lightning, which was his enemy, he makes a friend which does his errands for him. Steam, which was a stranger to him, he makes a slave to do his work for him, and carry him about; and long before he had advanced so far as this, animals which were hostile to him or indifferent to him were brought to serve him. Barren wastes under his influence became fertile fields. He crossed mountains and deserts that had been impassable. He navigated seas upon which at one time he dared not have ventured, and upon which he could not have preserved his life in the least storm. He painted pictures, carved statues, built towns. He wove cloths, contrived tools, printed books. In all these ways, and in thousands more, we see man's active nature adjusting itself to the material universe in which man finds himself placed; for in all the material progress which man has made he created nothing, and did not so much alter nature as himself. Whoever will think of it will see that the advance essentially consisted in this, that man placed himself in favorable relations to forces which always existed. Although it is our habit to dwell more on the changes which man has effected in the outer world, and less on the changes which the outer world has effected in him, yet these last are the important changes, and not the first. Man, in his savage state, was, by his active nature, in relation with only a few forms of mechanical force and a few forms of heat. At present, man's active relations with motion are immeasurably greater than then. His relations with heat, through steam, the smelting furnace, the rolling mill, and innumerable other processes and industries, are enormously extended. His active nature has entered into relations with light—for instance, through photography, and with the chemical forces in thousands of processes in which he avails himself of the agency of these, as in dyeing, many mining processes, and pharmacy. Man is also establishing relations between his active nature and magnetism, as, for instance, in the compass, the various uses of the magnet, and the thermo-multiplier. But still we know that with all these relations established this copartnership is only in its infancy. There are probably forces with which we have as yet formed no relationship. Who dreamed of electricity, magnetism, chemical affinity, or of light as forces in the Stone Age? and with those mentioned innumerable other relationships will undoubtedly be formed, of which we as yet have no conception. But the central fact in this storm of action which alone is important to us here, and which I wish to make plain, is this, that all the advance made by man in his direct relation with the external world through his active nature has been necessarily justified by and made possible by the forces of that external world; and that the hope of any further progress which he may look to make in the same direction must rest upon a belief, beyond all doubt well founded, in the existence of phases of force with which he may yet put himself in relation, and which will justify and render possible a further advance. We all of us, in fact, believe that the inter-relationship between man's active nature and the forces of the outside world is practically in its possibilities unlimited. That the external world is prepared to justify and support any conceivable advance in the same direction in which man's active nature has advanced in the past—that man's active development may take in the future.

A parallel statement regarding man's intellectual nature would be also true. This in its early crude state was forced into contact with the phenomena and relations which exist in nature, and a knowledge of the more obvious and simple of them was acquired. Ideas of number, form, size, distance, movement; of the sun, moon, stars; of heat, cold, hunger, and thirst; of pleasure and pain; love and hate; life and death. The order in which vague ideas became condensed into definite knowledge need not be discussed here. All that we want to see is that by means of his intellectual nature man has placed himself more and more *en rapport* with the facts and laws of the universe; that his intellect covers or tallies a constantly increasing surface in space and time, and constantly tallies it more and more accurately. That is to say, man's intellect becomes more and more completely moulded on and adapted to the external world— is brought more and more into correspondence with it. We also have good reason to think that our intellectual nature has so far only come into relation with an infinitely small proportion of the facts and laws of the universe. That we are like children gathering a few handfuls of shells on the sea-shore, while the vast ocean of truth stretches before us almost untouched. We have reason to think that the facts and laws of the universe would justify even an infinite advance in the direction which our intellectual nature has travelled in the past and is travelling to-day— that as force is infinite, so law is infinite.

Is there any reason to suppose that the same thing is not true of the moral nature and that aspect of the outer world with which it corresponds? Which moral nature, that of an animal, of a savage, of an average civilized man, the highest moral nature we know, or the moral sense of a being infinitely higher in the scale of creation than any of these—which moral sense of all these shall we believe to be the one which gives the most faithful account of the truth and value to us of the universe? Which is the truest mirror and reflects this aspect of the outer world most faithfully? We know that the best active nature, that which is the last evolved, tallies force less incompletely, tallies a larger part of its surface than a more incomplete and earlier active nature; and that it is therefore a truer index of force in its entirety than a less perfect active nature. We have every reason to believe also that there are forms of force which our active nature has not yet come into relationship with, but with which it will probably some day enter into relationship when it has still further developed. And there is no doubt whatever that it will enter into more complete relationship in the future than it has yet done with those forces such as motion, heat, and electricity, with which a relationship is already established. It will then tally more truly than it does now with this aspect of the fact of the external world. We also believe that an infinite progression in this line would be necessary to tally all the variety of forces in their infinite diversity and combination, and that therefore an infinite progression would be required to complete the fullest development of the active nature which the forces or force of nature would allow.

So we know that our intellectual nature tallies the facts and laws of the universe more completely now than it did in the past. We see, in this field, from the nature of the case, far more clearly than in the other two corresponding fields, that it is the fact of the universe being outside us and being as it is which makes possible, justifies, and proves this advance. We see also here more clearly than elsewhere that if man continues to live under the same conditions as heretofore his intellectual nature must continue to advance in the same direction which it has followed in the past. We see that before man's intellectual nature shall fully cover the phenomena and relations of the universe an infinite advance in its present course will have to be made. That, in fact, the external world has justified what has been done, and is able to justify an infinite advance in the same direction. Though we cannot, from the nature of the case, see it in the same clear manner, the same thing must be true of the moral nature and its correlative in the external world. A certain advance in a certain line has been made. That advance we are satisfied is justified. Every one sees that it is. No one thinks, or can think, that his love and faith are not, on the whole, justified. Everything tends to show that a further advance in the same line will be made, and that just as certainly as made it will be justified. Supposing that an infinite advance be made in the same line, will not it also be justified? In other words, hate and fear are dying out. The argument is that their total extinction is justified. Faith and love are increasing. Infinite faith and love are justified. That means that there is nothing to warrant fear and nothing to warrant hate in the universe. It also means that the real nature of the universe is such that it warrants on our part unlimited love and absolute trust. Why, then, if we live in a world where everything is really good and beautiful, and in which an all-powerful and infinitely beneficent providence holds us safe through life and death in its keeping forever, why should we ever fear? Why should we ever hate? For the same reason that, living in a world of infinite possibilities of action, we toil like slaves for a poor reward, the means of a bare subsistence. For the same reason that, living in a world of infinite law and order, we grope in the dark through the centuries for scraps of knowledge. For the reason that our moral nature, like our intellectual and active natures, is bound in seven-fold adamantine chains, so that we cannot love, cannot trust, just as we cannot act, cannot know, even to the extent that our petty intellects tell us we ought, like the half-grown boy, who, though he has learned not to believe in ghosts, still trembles in the dark. This is no new theory. We all recognize, and have recognized all along, that this is so, that the highest moral nature is nearest in accord with the truth of things. This is why we call those men inspired who have the most exalted moral natures, and those men wise who have exceptionally exalted moral natures as well as superior intellectual natures, and give the man with merely the superior intellectual nature and a mediocre moral nature the lower title of clever, and the man with a good intellectual nature and a low moral nature we call merely sharp or cunning. This is why we rank a man of genius, that is, a man whose greatness essentially consists in moral elevation, above a man of talent, that is, a man who is great by his intellect alone or by his intellect chiefly.

We see, then, do we not, that religion, morality, and happiness are three names for the same thing—moral elevation.

This, then, is the end, the conclusion of the whole matter: Love all things—not because it is your duty to do so, but because all things are worthy of your love. Hate nothing. Fear nothing. Have absolute faith. Whoso will do this is wise; he is more than wise—he is happy.

www.ingramcontent.com/pod-product-compliance
Lightning Source LLC
Chambersburg PA
CBHW031829230426
43669CB00009B/1281